2010

Recovery NOW!

K Lopher

R A Patu

Thanks from
QAD

I don't have to dwell on the point that cars mean more to these kids than
architecture did in Europe's great formal century, say, 1750 to 1850.
They are freedom, style, sex, power, motion, color – everything is right there.

Tom Wolfe, *The Kandy-Kolored Tangerine-Flake Streamline Baby*, 1964.

First published in 2008 by Conran Octopus Ltd,
a part of Octopus Publishing Group,
2–4 Heron Quays, London E14 4JP
www.octopusbooks.co.uk

An Hachette Livre UK Company
www.hachettelivre.co.uk

British Library Cataloguing-in-Publication Data.
A catalogue record for this book is available from
the British Library.

Publisher: Lorraine Dickey
Managing Editor: Sybella Marlow
Copy Editor: Sian Parkhouse

Art Direction and Design: Jonathan Christie
Photographer: Tif Hunter
Photographer's Producer: Sue Allatt
Picture Researcher: Anne-Marie Hoines

Production Director: Frances Johnson
Production Manager: Katherine Hockley

ISBN: 978 1 84091 504 4

CARS

FREEDOM
STYLE
SEX
POWER
MOTION
COLOUR
EVERYTHING

STEPHEN BAYLEY
ORIGINAL PHOTOGRAPHY BY TIF HUNTER

conran
OCTOPUS

Everywhere,
Giant finned cars nose forward like fish;
A savage servility
Slides by on grease.

Robert Lowell, *For the Union Dead*, 1964.

Automobiles are hollow, rolling sculpture. They have interior spaces corresponding to an outer form, like buildings, but the designer's aesthetic purpose is to enclose the functioning parts of an automobile, as well as its passengers, in a package suggesting directed movement along the ground.

Arthur Drexler, 1951.

This is not a book about cars.

At least, not in the sense of technology, production engineering, crash-testing, environmental impact, dynamics or motor racing. It is not about industry or manufacturing. You will find no references to power outputs, speed, acceleration… nor hardly any to cost.

It is not about the sport of driving, the endocrine rush of going snick-snick-snick through the gears as the neck muscles tighten, the exhaust parps and the landscape blurs. Nor is it about the mundane torment of commuting in serial tedium. It is not about the raw data – the economics, the beans, the counters – that once made cars America's primary product. My subject is the more elusive one of art.

Because, ultimately, it was art that really made the car America's primary product. And later Europe's, then Japan's. The pioneer of management consultancy, Alfred McKinsey, believed that everything can be measured. And he based a whole business system (one that still corrupts manufacturers and governments) on the ancillary belief 'if you can measure it, you can manage it'. But art is as notoriously resistant to both measurement and management as it is powerful in its effect. From the moment car manufacturers discovered art in the 1920s, there have been attempts to manage it, to systematize it, but none has been successful. Even in an industry as hierarchical and stratified as automobile manufacturing, the great cars have been products of creative genius – aberrant, cussed, irreverent – not of scientific management. These great cars are, with pop and the media, our age's singular contribution to cultural history. The '57 Chevrolet Bel Air is at least as interesting as a '57 David Smith… with the added significance that it sold more. No formula exists to calculate aesthetic impact, but my feeling is that the Chevy – in the general scheme of things – outperforms the gallery sculpture.

This is a book about the 80 or so greatest car designs ever, the ones that changed the conventional wisdom, lifted the game, raised the bar. At five minutes to midnight for the heat engine, it is a book with an elegiac quality since it was the very opportunities and constraints offered by Karl Otto's four-stroke cycle that established the architecture of that wonderful, unique expression of human genius we know as 'the car'. The suck-bang-squeeze-blow of the Otto cycle will soon be history, but its legacy is still here to be enjoyed. Nothing, not even a building, has more passion, expertise and cunning put into its design. This is a book about cars as purely magical objects.

But it is not a book about Figoni & Falaschi, Capron, Labourdette, de Villars, Letournour et Marchand, H.J. Mulliner and Franay. These were some of the great coachbuilders, artisan firms that sculpted metal into liquid, languid forms on aristocratic chassis. Such was Jay Gatsby's Rolls-Royce (yellow with green leather upholstery). Of these coachbuilt masterpieces there were rarely duplicates: a coachbuilt car was as singular as a Poiret couture gown. Certainly, Scott Fitzgerald used a Rolls-Royce as a motif which said several things about its owner's social mobility. But this is not a book about fabulous one-offs.

Introduction
Nature builds no machines

Opposite: Car design turns raw materials into a means of expression. This is Renault's steel stockyard, photographed by company photographer Robert Doisneau, in 1935. Soon, billets and sheets will become sculpture.

Instead, it is about cars that were produced in series (even if, in the case of some Ferraris and Lamborghinis, that series was very short and relied to a large extent on craft techniques). This is a book about cars as the ultimate product of consumerized industrial capitalism. It is about mass production. Le Corbusier said mass production leads to standards, and standards lead to perfection. Few cars ever were or are perfect, except for that brief moment when they are brand new and, for that quantum of time (before they are scratched, get dirty or become obsolete) when they are the ultimate that art and industry can contrive. At least, until next year.

By about 1901, the fundamental architecture of the car had been established by Daimler's 'Mercedes' (although here's a clue to the way development was going: Mercedes was named after a girl, the daughter of a Daimler importer). There were four wheels. There were usually four passengers, one of them behind the wheel (although at the very first it was a tiller). One of Dr Otto's internal combustion engines was mounted front or rear. Sometimes there might be just two passengers. The bodywork might be open, like a buggy, or closed like a State Coach. (The car vocabulary includes words such as 'berlinetta' and 'limousine', derived from old coaching types, themselves inspired by urban destinations). At first, the car resembled what was quite literally a horseless carriage, but as the technology became more familiar, as cars became more democratically accessible, no longer aristocratic playthings, artistry began to intervene.

Over the years shown in this book, this nearly inflexible architecture has inspired astonishing formal inventiveness by designers. Within a grid as fixed as the classical orders, metal (and occasionally, plastic) has been hammered, bent, pressed, stretched, perforated, chromed and painted in pursuit of emotional expression. The range of proportion and expression attainable seems unlimited. People who say 'all cars tend to look the same' are people who do not have eyes to see. The variety and ingenuity astonishes while, commensurately, the disciplines are intense. Car designers learn to work within astonishing constraints, not just of technology, but of aesthetics, too. There is only a few millimetres' difference, Jaguar designer Geoff Lawson once explained, between a curve that is fat and a curve that is anorexic. Without books to teach them, car designers have learnt a potent formal language: how one radius can convey strength, another weakness. They learn also about meaningful detail, the psychology of colour, proportion and the way light falls on surfaces. And they pass on these lessons to consumers.

Renaissance sculptors had similar skills and practised them with comparable science. In his treatise *De Statua,* Leon Battista Alberti has tables (Tabulae Dimensonium Hominis) where he publishes average, or ideal, dimensions for each component and sector of the body. 'Ad os, sub quo pendet penis' for example, which may be best left untranslated. The language of car design is just as sophisticated, but more demanding, since it operates on so large a scale. And it has to take into account not just the stern disciplines of cost, but also the ineluctable vagaries of taste.

Like all other designers, only more so, the car designer has to live in the future. This means, in effect, that when a brand-new car appears on the market, the designers have probably already designed the successor of its successor. This form of time-travel tests any complacent assumptions about novelty and fashion. The car designer's task is to dream, but in a practical way: he deals in fantasies measurable in millimetres and anchored by budgets and fickle consumer whim. So, at the same time, they have to conceive a package that excites the consumer's cupidity… but not by an alienating amount.

One of the founders of the industrial design profession was Raymond Loewy (whose postwar Studebaker Starliner, a car that brought European style to the United States, had an influence wildly out of proportion to its commercial significance). Loewy liked to talk about the MAYA principle, or 'Most Advanced Yet Acceptable', a sort of portion-control system for the distribution of creativity between client and customer. Ever since, car designers constantly test the limits of MAYA. Sometimes, as with Patrick Le Quément's Renault Avantime, they create a vehicle of audacious conceptual originality, a sort of intergalactic day-van coupé, which fails because it tests the public too much. But the most successful cars have the MAYA principle in correct balance… leaving just enough room for next year's model. 'Go all the way and then come back some,' Harley Earl told his designers in Detroit. Very often they did not bother to come back much, as the '59 Cadillac shows. This car may be many things, good and bad, but what is indisputable and what fascinates is that here is an extreme of human creativity. The cars were as inflated as the names. Eldorado Brougham – possibly, in some variants, Eldorado Brougham Seville – sounds today like a spoof version of Indiana Jones with a public school accent.

Antoine Laumet de la Mothe Cadillac was the French trader-adventurer who founded Fort Pontchartrain du Detroit. 'Detroit' means 'straight', although nothing could be more exaggerated, baroque, overwrought or visually complicated than Detroit's primary product at its economic peak. The '59 Cadillac is an engineering atrocity, viewed in the purist terms that, say, Dr Porsche would understand. To admonish its designers for their head-butting assault on the environment is as sensible as reprimanding a fish for being wet. The '59 Cadillac was created in a world where (at least) Americans knew no constraints of appetite, whose ambitions of comfort and desire and fantasy were regularly refreshed by corporations that had ample funds to do so. It is the most absurd, magnificent, appalling and perfect demonstration of consumerism without morals. Of course, the cars were as inflated as the names. The Germans called the phenomenon 'Detroit Machiavellismus'. But as Machiavelli insisted, the end result was what mattered. And if the end result was cruising down the freeway in a bright pink Cadillac, here was a rational solution.

As a result of this mixture of creativity and discipline, always addressed to the customer's ambitions and aspirations, cars soon acquired powerful symbolic character. The car is no less than the single most significant

Cars, cars, fast, fast! One is seized, filled with enthusiasm, with joy… the joy of power. The simple and naive pleasure of being in the midst of power, of strength.

Le Corbusier, *The City of Tomorrow*, 1929.

manufactured object. In America the automobile became, in a country where invention became the mother of necessity, a useful demonstration of Nathaniel Hawthorne's principle that wealth is the only true measure of rank. In Europe, with its more nuanced class system, cars were more often a measure of something other than wealth. But whatever your personal status or style, your car became an extension of your ego. Indifference is not an option. The person who declares, 'I'm not interested in cars, I just drive an old Volvo' is merely confirming what a powerful symbolic statement a Volvo makes, especially if it has acquired the automobile equivalent of bottle age.

The evolution of car design is a story of fantastic artistry and inventiveness. Within the simple constraints of the unchanging architecture of the automobile, its wheels, seats and engine, metal and plastic and glass have been tormented and teased to express 'freedom, style, sex, power, motion, color, everything'. In terms of aesthetics, it is a story of how the disparate forms of the primitive horseless carriage became integrated into a sculptural whole. But then the story rapidly evolves so that the same sculptural whole both interprets and, later, directs consumer psychology. As soon as car designers had, circa 1927, come to discover the sculptural possibilities of the mass-produced car, it was a moment of change in culture. The Bible, books, architecture, gallery art, popular ornaments all suddenly became subsidiary to car design as concessions to popular aesthetic curiosity. Only rock music and the movies (with which the car has so very much in common) can compare with the cultural impact of the designed automobile. She meant it ironically, but the town-planning critic Jane Jacobs was entirely correct to say that by about 1960, the purpose of American life was to use and consume automobiles.

Besides the sculptural inventiveness which made the consumer's cupidity itch, there is the philosophical idea of personal mobility embodied by the car. And, of course, ideas about mobility are fundamental to the liberal democracies where the car first flourished. This germ of freedom may be ineradicable from our understanding of what a car can be (even as day-to-day conditions from Bangkok to Los Angeles mock the genie of freedom whom Henry Ford helped escape from his bottle on a Michigan farm). In his magnificent essay 'From Sea to Shining Sea' (published in 1953, but describing events that took place 31 years before) the *New Yorker* journalist E. B. White describes his six-month transcontinental trip from New York to Seattle in a Model T Ford. No one has ever better captured the almost lascivious thrill of (or at least of anticipating) a car journey:

'Everything lay ahead, and we had plenty of time of day: the land stretched interminably into the West and into the imaginations of young men. Our car seemed full of a deep inner excitement, just as we did ourselves. The highway was a blazed trail of paint-rings on telegraph poles, a westering trace marked by arrows whittled out of shingles and tacked negligently to the handiest tree.'

Above: The car gave freedom to a generation of consumers hitherto confined to urban life. At the same time, it altered for ever the relationship between town and country. Robert Doisneau's picturesque 'Dejeuner sur l'herbe', 1935.

Below: Even in the computer age, car designers use sculptural techniques a medieval mason would have recognized. A designer in Wolfsburg is working on a clay model of the Volkswagen Polo, 1984.

Confident of his Ford's reliability, White left his *Automobile Blue Book* behind and took for reading matter instead his Webster's *Unabridged Dictionary*. His true destination was not Seattle, but… the world of letters.

The car is an important and recurrent motif in American 20th-century literature, perhaps unsurprisingly for a nation more dependent on cars than Europe, in whose literature references to cars are less frequent and less portentous. Delmore Schwartz, author of the noirish *In Dreams Begin Responsibilities* drove a 1929 Chrysler Imperial, a car of much gravitas. 'The ego,' he maintained 'is always at the wheel.' Henry Miller had an even darker view. In *The Air-Conditioned Nightmare* (1945) he wrote, 'The automobile stands out as the very symbol of falsity and illusion.' But falsity and illusion are defining characteristics of movies, of art, of theatre, of literature. Falsity and illusion fascinate. Mastery of them requires genius.

So cars powered a lot of what is significant in contemporary culture. In 1951 a young roughneck called Ike Turner recorded 'Rocket 88' in Sam Philips's Sun Studios in Memphis, a song inspired by the '49 Oldsmobile. The Oldsmobile Rocket V8 engine was introduced that year. Inserted into a light model 88 body, it provided exceptional performance. The record was a surprise hit, and one of the first black records bought by white youth. Its success allowed Philips to underwrite Elvis Presley, one of the first white youths to sound like a black man. A song about a $2,170, 3,585lb car was the basis for rock'n'roll. To confirm the automobile's status in culture, the '49 Mercury starred in *Rebel Without a Cause*, the 1955 Nicholas Ray movie which allowed James Dean to make a poetic case for juvenile violence.

The Paris savant Roland Barthes made popular culture (including Marilyn Monroe and steak'n'chips) the subject of serious academic study in his Sorbonne seminars. He may not have been aware of the part Ike Turner and suburban Oldsmobile engineers played in the creation of rock's iconography, but he was most certainly aware of how in the twentieth century the car acquired extraordinary symbolic power. In the greatest

**No dignity without chromium
No truth but a glossy finish
If she purrs she's virtuous
If she hits ninety she's pure…**

William Carlos Williams, *Ballad of Faith*, 1954

essay on the automobile written by a European, Barthes said of the Citroën DS (in *Mythologies*, 1957), that 'cars are our cathedrals'. His intention was mischievous. But it was a serious observation, too. Both as technical achievements and as symbols of collective aspirations, the great churches of the Middle Ages and twentieth-century automobiles had much in common.

Seven years after Barthes, Tom Wolfe had another insight into the symbolic power of the car. Visiting a California drag strip for a magazine assignment, he realised Ford and Chevrolet were doing what Le Roi Soleil did at Versailles. Cars, Wolfe says, are tied up with religion and architecture, just like sculpture in the age of Benvenuto Cellini. In *The Kandy-Kolored Tangerine-Flake Streamline Baby*, he wrote, 'Cars mean more to these kids than architecture did in Europe's great formal century, say, 1750 to 1850. They are freedom, style, sex, power, motion, color – everything is right there.' There you have my title.

The story of car design begins in 1908, which Aldous Huxley called

'The Year of our Ford'. There is a famous and very bad photograph of Henry Ford labelled, almost biblically, 'The First Car'. He sits astride his ungainly gasoline buggy, the unlikely apparatus that freed peasant America, created the universal suburb, became an engine of wealth, destroyed the countryside, enslaved the world. The claim of the caption is not strictly true. Germans and Austro-Hungarians may have developed the technology of the car, but Henry Ford knew how to exploit it. The ordinary man's yearning for independence and freedom, in Ford's own case described as a pressing need to escape the crushing boredom of life on a Mid-West farm, was the basis of his appeal. Or what we today might call a brand proposition. At first, independence and freedom were defined in terms of physical mobility. Later, as design became more sophisticated, they became defined in terms of psychological expression, of desire.

This Ford was an epochal figure. An intuitive mechanical genius, a wizard of motivation, a plain-talking anti-Semite and anti-intellectual, a man

Opposite: The romance of the car was powerfully enhanced by celebrity accidents and none was more celebrated than James Dean's. Here he is at the wheel of a Porsche RSK just a few days before his death in a 1955 collision with a Ford truck in the California desert.

Above: Photographers often responded to the physical qualities of fine cars with their gorgeous shapes and lustrous sheens. This is Louis Faurer's almost abstract study of Cadillacs in a Park Avenue garage, New York, 1950.

obsessed with efficiency and technology, but sentimentally located in small-town America of the nineteenth century. In the third volume of *USA*, the one called *The Big Money* (1933), John Dos Passos devotes seven pages to Henry Ford, including this bravura passage:

> 'At Ford's production was improving all the time; less, waste, more spotters, strawbosses, stool-pigeons (fifteen minutes for lunch, three minutes to go to the toilet, the Taylorized speedup everywhere, reachunder, adjustwasher, screwdown bolt, shove in cotter pin, reachunder, adjustwasher, screwdown bolt, reachunderadjustscrewdownreachunderadjust, until every ounce of life was sucked off into production and at night the workmen went home gray shaking husks.'

Or maybe, eventually, they were fortunate enough to go home in a '49 Ford, a '57 Fairlane Skyliner or a '64 Mustang.

Henry Ford's cars eased Americans 'through the dislocations created by breathtaking historical change', at least according to Steven Watts in his book *The People's Tycoon* (2005). Ford was obsessed by process, not art. His company had a (pioneering, if sinister) sociological department and Ford said, 'We want to make men in these factories as well as cars.' The term 'Fordism' was coined to describe this totalitarian approach to labour (the very approach that drew Hitler to Ford).

Yet Ford and his family were not wholly resistant to the blandishments of art. In 1927 Ford hired hyper-realist painter Charles Sheeler to document the awesome River Rouge plant. *Vanity Fair* put the Ford factory's conveyors and tracks on its cover that year. Four years later, Henry's more sensitive son, Edsel B. Ford, somewhat incongruously commissioned Mexican communist painter Diego Rivera, lover of Frieda Kahlo, to paint industrial murals in the Detroit Institute of Arts that the Fords bankrolled.

But if the Ford achievement was in consumerizing mobility, its rival General Motors' achievement was, through the innovative medium of car design, in consumerizing dreams. Alfred Sloan wrote a memorandum in the early Twenties that speculated on whether appearance (it was not yet called styling or design) might be used as a competitive advantage, as a means of exciting the consumer into buying more cars.

It shortly became apparent that appearances could, indeed, be made to excite the customer. There was a time before cars were designed, but then came Harley Earl. This extraordinary personality was the first person to realize that cars went from A to Z, not merely to B. On the way they passed those seductive ideas of 'freedom, style, sex power, motion, color – everything'.

'Who do you think you are, Mr Earl?' went the line of the Fifties song. 'And how was it that you pinched my girl?' went the refrain. GM Styling staff had probably heard the song because they called their big, sharp-suited, bullying boss 'Misterearl' all in one word. So that is an answer to the first question. And a generation of movies culminating in George Lucas' 1973 *American Graffiti* answered the question asked in the refrain. Earl made cars sexy, among other attributes.

Thus it was Earl who gave the world some of its most potent modern symbols: the Detroit automobile of the high Fifties. These were cars to cruise in, although better adapted in many ways to the drive-in than to driving. Voluptuous curves, opulent paint, strange glass, lascivious chrome, pleated Naugahyde, bizarre symbolism. Yes, they were also cart-sprung barges with atrociously inefficient engines and no brakes. But if you can look at a '59 Cadillac, or even a humbler '59 Chevrolet Impala hardtop coupé (in Sunburst Yellow) and not feel a sense of heartbreaking antic larrikin wonder at the sheer, inflammatory wonder of it all, then you are reading the wrong book. In a world which allowed the '59 Impala to come into being, anything was possible.

Above: The Citroën 2CV – Pierre Boulanger's 'umbrella on wheels'.

Right: Zoltan Glass was an experimental Hungarian photographer who worked for Mercedes-Benz in the 1930s. Influenced by Bauhaus principles of design, his promotional photographs often used daring angles and radical compositions.

Opposite left: In America the automobile became a symbol of freedom as well as a symbol of the consumer's alienation in a vast, branded, mechanized world. 'All roads lead West' suggests a vista of endless possibility for this Buick parked by a drugstore.

Opposite right: The ravishing boat tail of a Mercedes-Benz Cabriolet photographed by Zoltan Glass at a Berlin Motor Show circa 1934. Hitler used the technocratic prestige of Mercedes-Benz as nationalist propaganda.

By raiding every iconographic source he could find, from fighter aircraft to rocket ships, the Santa Monica Raceway and rumba dancing, Earl gave form to the most vivid version of the American dream: a life made perfect by advanced consumerism. It is short-changing genius to say all he achieved was chrome baubles and tail fins. He gave America a mirror of its own ambitions. A US Secretary of Defense once said what was good for General Motors was good for America. When that verity crashed, the mirror cracked. Woodrow Wilson called the American car a picture of the 'arrogance of wealth'. Ah yes. I am writing this the very day Toyota overtook GM to become world number one.

Harley Earl was born in Hollywood on 22 November 1893, the son of J.W. Earl, a local coachbuilder making wagons, carriages and racing sulkies for the Mexican farmers who populated this part of California before the movies arrived. Ethel Barrymore described Hollywood as 'a glaring, gaudy, nightmarish set, built in the desert'. But that was later (after the Horsley Brothers rented a rundown tavern at Sunset and Gower and started making films using drunken actors). Earl grew up in a family that was, by shifting Californian standards, almost dynastically rooted: while his father had been a Michigan lumberjack, his mother was born there, daughter of a civil dignitary. They were prosperous, socially established and in a position to predict the coming of the private car, an event anticipated by the relaunch in 1908 of the family business as the Earl Automobile Works.

In the same year the movies began, Earl Automobile started making custom-made car bodies and fuselages for the Glen L. Martin Company, pioneers of Californian aerospace. Harley Earl's name first appeared in the newspapers in 1919 when the *Los Angeles Times* noted his spectacular bodywork at the local Auto Show. Clients soon included cowboy star Tom Mix and Fatty Arbuckle, for whom Earl made what he described as 'the most streamlined vehicle anywhere', although we would not see it that way. For Mix, in a gesture that established his ineffable taste for symbolic kitsch, Earl attached a saddle to the roof. While Henry Ford was mass-producing cost-effective black (it was nothing to do with aesthetics, black's thermal properties allowed rapid air-drying of paint), Earl had a comedian client pour cream in his coffee until it reached exactly the desired shade of brown. In these early designs, motifs that would later preoccupy Earl began to appear: he had an obsession about cars being ever longer, ever lower. He enjoyed sculpted transitions, not sharp abutments. The 'trunk' was once exactly that, a survivor from the days of the carriage trade: Earl did away with strap-on storage and integrated the boot into the body. He liked expressive details and he simply loved colour.

When Don Lee, the West Coast Cadillac distributor, bought the Earl Automobile Works, it gave Earl a direct contact with Alfred Sloan's new conglomerate of General Motors. This organization was a masterpiece of American capitalist improvisation. General Motors' twin objectives of profit and growth were established (and never questioned) by founders Sloan and his partners William C. Durant and Charles F. Kettering. From the Hyatt Roller Bearing Company and Guardian Frigerator Company grew GM's Detroit factoryscape and its five divisions, the first challenger to Ford's market dominance. While Raymond Chandler had said that Hollywood had 'all the character of a papercup', Detroit was an awe-inspiring spectacle. For Harley Earl it became a sort of theatre.

Demobbed US soldiers were ready for pleasure. 'How Ya Gonna Keep 'Em Down on the Farm (After They seen Paree)?' was a popular song, amply eloquent of how travel might enhance the expectations of boys fresh off the ranch. In his book *Only Yesterday*, Frederick Lewis Allen pointed out that while in 1913 a woman's dress required nearly 20 yards of fabric, by 1928 a typical dress required merely seven. But it was psyches as well as bodies that were laid bare.

Drive ten thousand miles across America and you will know more about the country than all the institutes of sociology and political science put together.

Jean Baudrillard, *America*, 1989

Earl was lured to the mid-West by Lawrence Fisher of the Cadillac Division. Alfred Sloan had mused first about styling in 1921 and by 1926 the idea that the appearance of cars might actually affect sales was beginning to ripen colourfully in his meticulous mind. One of the weapons GM used to attack Ford was market segmentation: Ford thought a single product would suffice, Sloan disagreed. Thus Earl's first job was to fill an ugly $1,700 gap between Buick and Cadillac. This appeared in March 1927 under the new brand of La Salle and caused a sensation. Although inspired by the coachbuilt Hispano-Suiza (which Earl called 'Hisso'), to American eyes its appearance was entirely new: sharp corners had been excluded in favour of curved junctions, disparate elements were unified into a pleasing whole and the entire silhouette had been lowered to express speed and suggest elegance. Later, Earl said that his first GM car was 'slab-sided, top heavy and stiff shouldered', but that was just another way of saying how far he had travelled to reach the '59 Cadillac.

Thrilled by popular response to La Salle, Sloan now decided to acquire the transmutational services of Harley Earl for all GM divisions. On 23 June 1927 (the very same year that Raymond Loewy opened shop in Manhattan and started streamlining pencil sharpeners), Sloan announced the creation of the Art and Color Section with Harley Earl at its head. Just as the paint was drying on the Art and Color signage, Ford's Model T went out of production. The story of popular car design had begun. Art and Color's first car, the 1929 'pregnant' Buick, was not a success, but it taught Earl one of his great organizing principles: you have to lead the public, but not by too much. This was what Loewy had called MAYA.

Earl's capture and training of the public's cupidity had its parallel in William van Alen's 1930 Chrysler Building, an astonishing demonstration of the new status of the automobile in America. It has a frieze of hubcaps halfway up the building. Lewis Mumford sternly said that it was 'inane romanticism, meaningless voluptuousness, void symbolism'. He might as well have been describing the adventure of car design: its inanity and voluptuousness might have alienated epicene academic commentators, but they utterly seduced the consumer.

In 1936 E.B. White explained that his perception of his home, both actually and metaphorically, was framed by a car's windscreen: 'My own vision of the land – my own discovery of it – was shaped, more than by any other instrument, by a Model T Ford.' But the primitive Ford's screen was a frame. A contemporary industrial innovation provided designers with a fresh, empty canvas and extended Earl's personal vocabulary of form: US Steel introduced the high-speed strip which by 1934 was providing sheet metal in 2.2m (7ft 4 in) widths. Suddenly, new sculptural possibilities were viable. Three years later, Earl renamed Art and Color 'Styling' and, thus, a new word entered the vocabulary of international business. Styling's first job was to invent 'dream cars', drivers of the US economy, avatars of desire. A GM sales committee paper of 1925 had established the need for

Above: The influential 'Eight Automobiles' exhibition ran at New York's Mueum of Modem Art, 28 August–11 November, 1951. Curated by the tastemaker, Arthur Drexler, it gave the world the expression 'rolling sculpture' and legitimized car design as an art form.

Below: Talbot-Lago T150SS, 1941. Unconstrained by the cost and technical disciplines of mass-production, coachbuilders such as Figoni & Falaschi were able to design astonishing shapes for one-off, handmade production.

an annual model change to keep demand moving and it was Earl's job to lure the consumer with new visual ideas. Literally, he had to design change. To its critics this became planned obsolescence, but to GM it was more positively known as the dynamic economy. Besides, as Earl later said when confronted about the sins of redundancy and waste, 'We have not depreciated these cars, we have appreciated your mind.'

The first dream car was the 1937 Buick Y Job. Like everything else credited to Earl, it was actually drawn by someone else (in this case by one George Snyder), but it was part of Earl's innovative method to realize his creative vision by a process of critique, recommendation and, quite often, intimidation. Draftsmen trembled when he toured the studios. The Y Job was positioned in front of the Zeitgeist, to test reaction. It featured power windows, lights, a roof. Curiously small 33cm (13in) wheels made it look low and urgent; a dramatically sculpted shape abandoned running boards. Earl used it as his personal car on his many visits to the Grosse Pointe Club, the Yondatega Club and the Country Club of Detroit.

Passenger car production stopped in the Second World War, but Earl's vaulting imagination was not hindered by the diversion of global conflict. Quite the opposite, in fact. Here there were opportunities. GM's Allison Division supplied engines to Lockheed, whose P-38, sketched by Clarence L. ' Kelly' Johnson to a 1937 US Army Air Corps specification, was one of the most formally inventive and radical aircraft shapes. In 1942 Earl and his staff drove to Selfridge AFB to view one. Although not allowed any closer than 9m (30ft), it was enough to be inspiring. The projectile nose, the cockpit greenhouse, the beautifully contoured fuselage and (especially) the twin tail booms. Earl had found the symbolic source of car styling for the next decade: those booms inspired vestigial tail fins on the '48 Cadillac. Oldsmobile followed in '49 (the car Ike Turner so admired), Buick in '52, Chrysler in '55. Ford held out on tail fins until 1957, but by '59 the GM tail fin had evolved to the fantastical excess of the Impala. By the time Earl's infamous tail fins had trickled down from the apex of Cadillac to the base of Chevrolet, in full conformity with the laws of planned obsolescence the Cadillac of the following year appeared as a model of poise and restraint.

There were many great cars produced by GM under Harley Earl: the '53 Corvette, the '57 Bel Air, the ineffable '59 Cadillac. Each one glorious, but Earl's distinctive achievement was not so much individual vehicles (which were always a team effort), nor details… although the fins, chrome, two-tone paint, wraparound windscreens and twin headlights are all in his portfolio. Rather, it was to appreciate the structural significance of design and to institutionalize it. He invented the practices still used today: concept cars shown at spectacular presentations called 'Motoramas', clay modelling, platform sharing and brand separation. He called design 'thinking out loud' and insisted that the designer's role was to give the customer a 'visual receipt' for his dollars. He knew it was the entertainment business, citing his one-time neighbour Cecil B. De Mille's theatricality and Al Jolson's

way with an audience as inspirations. 'You can design a car so that every time you get in it, it's a relief – you have a little vacation for a while' was a mantra.

And throughout the period Tom Wolfe called 'America's Bourbon Louis romp' it all worked perfectly. As one Yale physicist put it, the Chevrolet Division of GM alone was at one point offering so many different body styles, engine options, transmission variants, trim colours, paints and accessories that the available range seemed likely to exceed the number of atoms in the universe, thereby putting Harley Earl one step in front of God in the chain of command. But it was not just cars: Earl understood women as well. Somewhat a social conservative, not to say dinosaur, he conceded 'American women have a lot to say about what they want in the new family car.' Accordingly, in 1958 he raided the Pratt Institute for recruits to his new Saarinen-designed Tech Center in Warren. They provided a fashion show that drilled taproots so deeply into the American consumer psyche that they made a mere Motorama seem like disinterested scientific research.

As cars became cleaner and more reliable, woman became involved. First as customers (who were promised temporary liberation from dream kitchens), then, in a bizarre before-its-time episode, as designers. WASPS to a woman, these Vanderbilts and Fords were his 'Damsels of Design'. One Ruth Glennie did a Corvette which with pre-Freudian naivety she called 'Fancy Free' with silver, olive and white leather trim and slip covers to change with the seasons. Jeanette Linder had fitted fibreglass luggage in her Chevrolet Impala, pastel-striped to match the upholstery. Not satisfied with the manufacturer's ample provision of names for the Cadillac Eldorado Seville, Sue Vanderbilt proposed a Baroness version in subdued colours to 'permit the occupant to shine'. It had a black mouton carpet, a telephone and black seal-fur pillows and lap robe for rear passengers. Marjorie Ford, expressing heaven-knows-what psychic urges, had binoculars and camera fitted to a padded compartment in her Buick. 'I think in three or four years,' Earl cheerfully said, 'women will be designing [pause] entire automobiles.'

Never has a designer had as much power and influence and profile as Harley Earl. He wore cinnamon and sky blue linen suits, and kept changes of clothes in his office. He flew on the inaugural flight of the Boeing 707 and was filmed eating a banana. At design reviews he would lounge in chairs and point to details with the toe cap of a highly polished wingtip loafer. People said he lived as if he were auditioning for the role of the most unforgettable person you ever met. After he retired from GM on 1 December 1959, Earl set up a design consultancy, one of whose products was aerosol batter for Nabisco. He was not great with language (getting far too many syllables into the pronunciation of 'aluminum'), but he had an absolute genius for automobile art.

For example, Earl's policy of lengthening and lowering was so consistently applied that by 1954 a design weakness had been exposed: cars had dull, boring roofs, flat, undecorated areas of metal doing nothing but keep the weather out and the doors apart. His solution to visual ennui?

Two generations of Americans know more about the Ford coil than the clitoris, about the planetary system of gears than the solar system.

John Steinbeck, *Cannery Row*, 1945

'We grooved it.' Grooved it he did, for 32 years. When his career began, the car was a consumer novelty. By the time he was through with it, the car had become industrial civilization's premier product. He died in 1969. Not a bookish man, Earl said, 'I like baseball, but I love automobiles.'

Europe had no equivalent to Harley Earl and General Motors, and car design there developed rather differently. While Americans were thrilling to the wholesome discovery of fresh horizons, the more complex presence of sexual elements in the culture of the car were noted first in Europe. Playwright Alfred Jarry (remembered mostly for a play whose first line was 'Merde!') spoke with deliberate ambiguity about the 'immodest organ of propulsion'. The Futurist poet and pamphleteer Filipo Tommaso Marinetti said: 'I became inflamed with the fever and desire of the steely breaths from your full nostrils! I finally unleash your metallic bride… you launch yourself, intoxicatingly into the liberating infinite.' Was he addressing his car or his mistress? Or both? It is a positional dilemma still known today.

The Dada artist Francis Picabia found occult erotica in car technology. He analyzed and made montages from technical illustrations, labelling them suggestively to reveal the hilarious, but profound, association between lubricated, mechanical moving parts and the muscle, gristle and mucus of love. One such is *L'Enfant Carburateur* of 1919, in which a humble Claudel carburettor is invested with the erotic power of Titian's *Venus of Urbino*. Picabia notes the common ground between the Otto-cycle and sex encapsulated in the word reciprocation. He smirks about valve guides, an equivalent, surely, of the female sheath. An annotation by Picabia of a technical drawing says 'Dissolution of Prolongation', which means so little and so much.

Yet, while it has often been said that sex is used to sell cars, there are several notorious examples where it failed to do anything of the sort. In 1923 Ned Jordan wrote the copy for an advertisement for his own Jordan Playboy runabout. It appeared in the Saturday *Evening Post* of 23 June 1923 and must stand as some sort of masterpiece of unconscious camp:

> 'Somewhere west of Laramie, there's a bronco-busting, steer-roping girl who knows what I'm talking about. She can tell what a sassy pony, that's a cross between greased lightning and the place where it hits, can do with eleven hundred pounds of steel and action when he's going high wide and handsome.'

As a result of this sordid, puerile, imagistic drivel – 'she loves the cross of the wild and the fame – a hint of old loves – and saddle and squirt' – sales declined from 6,691 in 1923 to 6,159 the following year.

e.e. cummings' poem 'She being Brand', Number XIX in his collection *Is 5* (1926), was written at the moment the management at General Motors was beginning to appreciate that, with design and consumer psychology applied, respectively, to the manufacture and sales of the automobile, it could be translated from a practical, but rattling, contraption to a dream machine.

In his signature fragmented and anarchic style, cummings expresses the adventure of driving wonderfully. His terms of reference are those of both a consumer and a lover. The opening passage makes deliberate play between a brand-new car being stiff (and needing to be run-in) and the conquest of virgin flesh. Like Picabia, cummings knows that, given the context he has so clearly established, an expression such as 'thoroughly oiled' is ambiguous:

> Oh and her gears being in
> A1 shape passed
> From low through
> Second-in-to-high like
> Greasedlightning) just as we turned the corner of Divinity

For cummings and, indeed, his readers, the in and out motions of the clutch and the car's juddering progress are a lyrical diagram of, first, deflowering which then becomes cooperative pleasure:

> Internalexpanding
> &
> externalcontracting

ending, happily, in the shared, nerveless Nirvana of satisfaction

> brought allofher tremB
> -ling
> to a : dead.
> Stand-
> ;Still)

For a certain genre of American authors, cars remained powerful symbols of sex in all its shapes, sizes and opportunities. In *V* (1964) Thomas Pynchon has, at the dawn of the feminist revolution, the woman in charge. In this case, of her MG (possibly an MGA, the author is not specific):

> '"You beautiful stud," he heard her say, "I love to touch you." What, he thought. "Do you know what I feel when we are out on the road? Alone, just us?" She was running the sponge caressingly over its front bumper "Your funny responses, darling, that I know so well. The way your brakes pull a little to the left, the way you start to shudder around 5000rpm when you're excited."'

The best European manufacturers and designers tended to be more concerned with the explicitly artistic and creative aspects of car design. Few companies have enjoyed a better reputation for design excellence, not to say wanton eccentricity, than Citroën. From the start, Andre Citroën

We shall learn to be masters rather than servants of nature.

Henry Ford, 1922

I regard Henry Ford as my inspiration.

Adolf Hitler, *The Detroit News*, 31 December 1931

Right: The style of a country's roads reflects a nation's preoccupations as accurately as the cars that drive upon them. This is the Pacific Coast Highway, US1: vast, magnificent, unpredictable.

invested creative beliefs and ideals in his manufacturing business. While this often frustrated conservative investors and bankers (indeed, resulting, some would say 'inevitably', in a 1934 bankruptcy), it also eventually produced what is, perhaps, the single most magical car design of them all: the Citroën DS.

Citroën's belief was that 'Dès l'instant qu'une idée est bonne, le prix n'a pas d'importance.' He also attached special significance to sales and promotion, which he turned into as vigorous an art form as car design itself. In 1929 Ilya Ehrenburg published his *Life of the Automobile*. Here he writes:

'In the old days, foreign and provincial tourists in Paris would hurry off to see the gargoyles of Notre Dame or the Mona Lisa. But today, the first thing they do is view the Citroën works.'

And, perhaps also, the Citroën showroom on Paris' Champs-Elysées where his cars were given the reverence due to museum pieces. After the bankruptcy, the tyre supplier Michelin, a leading creditor, acquired the

company. Citroën, a gambler in all aspects of life, died disappointed and broke one year later, but not before his principles had established a creative culture that led to a series of the most audacious designs ever seen.

The great Citroëns – the Traction Avant, the 2CV, the DS – were all the work of one man: Citroën's body designer, Flaminio Bertoni. He was a sculptor and a painter, with links to late Surrealism and Medardo Rosso (the 'Impressionist' sculptor whose lifelike work was admired by Emile Zola) – but the crucial event in his life was his move from Italy to Paris in 1932 to work for a Citroën subcontractor. On 27 April he was hired by Andre Citroën himself. During a single night in 1934 Bertoni designed, using a sculptor's tools, the bodywork for the Traction Avant, the car that was Citroën's manifesto. As if to confirm that life in the car design studio was not separate from art in the atelier, in the very same year as he sculpted the Traction Avant, Bertoni exhibited at the 46eme Exposition des Beaux-Arts at Asnières.

Bertoni's next project for Citroën was the TPV ('Toute Petite Voiture'), an exercise in automobile Existenzminimum that was the French equivalent of Dante Giacosa's FIAT 500 and Dr Porsche's Volkswagen. Hitler's war (much

The motorcar... broke up family life, or so it seemed, in the Twenties. It separated work and the domicile, as never before. It exploded each city into a dozen suburbs... the motorcar ended the countryside.

Marshall McLuhan, *Understanding Media*, 1964

aided by Porsche designs for the Leopard tank (this was Porsche Typ 734, a post-War design) and the Vergeltungswaffe, better-known to Blitzed Londoners as the V-1 buzz-bomb) postponed production of the TPV, but in 1949 (after delays which caused wags to suggest the abbreviated name stood for 'Toujours Pas Vue') Bertoni's radical design was launched as the 2CV, which became the beloved *deux chevaux*. Surviving sketches in Bertoni's hand show a Bauhaus purity in the geometry, explicit industrial finishes and a bracing minimalism. In the same year he designed the 2CV, Bertoni exhibited with Giorgio de Chirico at Paris' Salon d'Automne.

In 1938 the Citroën company began work on its greatest ever project, 'VGD' (Voiture de Grand Diffusion). The creative brief was 'Study all the possibilities, including the impossible', which those involved did so very diligently. The result – a magnificent reconciliation of new materials and technology with audacious, sculptural curves and minimalist instrumentation – was the 1955 DS, the car which inspired Barthes. In order that consumers might best appreciate its dramatic form uncompromised by the encumbrance of wheels and tyres, the DS was first shown at the Paris Salon de l'Automobile

mounted on a pylon. With a phonic slip, it became the Déesse, and the Goddess became the most remarkable and admired car design of all time.

Although Bertoni was a native Italian, his work as a car designer was wholly in France and entirely French in flavour. The Italian tradition of car design was different from the French and, indeed, from any other national school, being sourced not in manufacturing or technology, but in the old trade of the *carrozzeria*, or coachbuilder. Their names are legion: Alessio, Allemano, Balbo, Bertone, Boano, Boneschi, Castagna, Fissore, Frua, Ghia, Michelotti, Moretti, Scaglietti, Touring, Vignale, Viotti and Zagato.

But the greatest of these is Pininfarina. The company history is needlessly complicated, but Stabilimenti Farina existed from 1905–1953. It was one of the first *carrozzerie* to use metal pressing and the informal academy where such figures as Mario Revelli de Beaumont, Pietro Frua and Giovanni Michelotti were first understudies, then studio masters. In 1930–1 Battista or 'Pinin' Farina established Carrozzeria Pininfarina SpA at via Lesna 78/80 in the Grugliasco district of Turin. The achievements of Pininfarina – as it evolved from artisan metal-bashing to high automobile art – are a

Opposite: FIAT's Lingotto factory in Turin was designed by engineer Giacomo Matte-Truco and built 1920–1923. A hugely ambitious concrete structure, in full conformity with Futurist art theory (which lionized speed), it featured an audacious test track on the roof.

Above: Volkswagen Beetles and Transporters at the Bremen docks, 18 February, 1966. The one designed by an Austrian engineer, the other by a Dutch entrepreneur, each became a symbol of Germany's Wirtschaftswunder.

summary of the immense Italian contribution to the history of car design.

In *Nato con l'automobile* (1968), the young Farina explained how he liked to polish his mother's casseroles. This was not so much an expression of filial piety, more an admission of an intuitive love of form and finish so influential on the Italian approach to manufactured objects. For an Italian, the expression *bella figura* – meaning a love of comportment and presentation and attention to detail – has real meaning in the way that 'good manners' used to in England.

The method of the Pininfarina *carrozzeria*, as with all others, was to work outside and alongside the manufacturers, presenting, in the early days, new bodies on established chassis, later presenting fully worked-up concept cars (developed at their own expense) created to lure and seduce manufacturers into lucrative design contracts. The *carrozzerie*, therefore, worked more as independent consultants, although close loyalties with manufacturers soon evolved for the most successful of them. In 1931 Pininfarina showed bodywork based on Alfa Romeo, Lancia and FIAT chassis at the Paris Salon de l'Automobile, but a distinctive design language did not emerge until the 1932 FIAT 518 Ardita, a roadster with elegantly flowing lines. Three years later, with the Alfa Romeo 6c Pescara, that emergent language had become clearly established. The year after, an extravagant 'Berlinetta aerodinamica' for Lancia predicted the sculptural glories of the Fifties. This was more than mere formal language; it was literature of a high order.

Commercial activity resumed after the war in 1946, but the defeated Italians were not allowed to exhibit at the influential Paris Salon de l'Automobile, so Pinin and his son Sergio simply parked an example of their work – actually a Lancia Aurelia Bilux – outside the Grand Palais and watched with delight as visitors took note.

The 1947 Cisitalia was the Pininfarina design that established a reputation that has endured. Cisitalia was an idiosyncratic business of no very great industrial significance, but its most famous car was celebrated in its day and has become an acknowledged masterpiece in the history of industrial design. Or some would quibble and say its historiography. Whatever, the Pininfarina-bodied Cisitilia 212 is a yearningly beautiful bargain between manufacturing and art, with elements of sport, opportunism and machismo included. It was shown at the Fiera di Milano and at the Coppa d'Ora di Villa d'Este in September, then, triumphantly, in Paris in November. At the Salon de l'Automobile, Pininfarina now had its own stand, where the Cisitalia starred, as if to establish its parity with manufacturers. The Cisitalia appearing at the Grand Palais – austere, but voluptuous and perfectly formed – was the same type chosen four years later for exhibition in New York's Museum of Modern Art. It was perhaps the very first time a whole car had been construed and executed as a sculptural whole. The Fifties followed.

Now Pininfarina became responsible for a series of cars that defined the age and gave to sheet steel or aluminium powers of expression hitherto

Above: Battista or 'Pinin' Farina standing next to his 'Florida II' show car – one of the most influential design proposals ever.

Below: The mid-Fifties was what Tom Wolfe described as America's 'Bourbon Louis romp', a moment of unprecedented and unreflective wealth. And nowhere did the American car flourish better than California. Magnum photographer Elliott Erwitt took this photograph in Hollywood, 1956.

reserved for marble. The Lancia B20 defined the 'GT', the original idea of a 'Grand Touring' car with all the attendant baggage of enlightenment travel, European trajectories and personal pleasure. Not to mention sophistication. Then in 1951 the Nash Healey Spider provided many of the styling cues that fed into the influential California Sports Car Cult. The following year, the epochal collaboration with Ferrari began.

The first car called a Ferrari appeared on 12 March 1947. Hitherto, Enzo Ferrari had managed the Alfa Romeo racing team, but his intractable ego and monumental conviction of self-worth could not be accommodated in anybody else's corporate structure. So he made his own. In an impoverished Italy of the *ricostruzione* this first Ferrari caused a sensation. It was made with total conviction and no concessions. The first race win (at the Rome Grand Prix of the same year) soon followed. The driver was one Franco Cortese (a gentleman amateur who sold the machine tools that Enzo Ferrari had manufactured during the Doppo Guerra Mondiale). I mention these details to illustrate the peculiar conditions of postwar Italy when Pininfarina began to thrive.

Between 1947 and 1951, inspired by V-12 Packards that raced at Indianapolis, Ferrari began the development of the glorious 12-cylinder engines which become his trademark. The first engine was designed by Gioachino Colombo, who was soon joined by Aurelio Lampredi from the aircraft manufacturer Officine Reggiane. To understand the drama of this, to appreciate Ferrari's classic bravura, Italy's bestselling car at the time, Dante Giacosa's FIAT Topolino, had a 500c twin-cylinder engine. In 1951 Ferrari said he felt as if he had killed his own mother when Argentinian racing driver Froilan Gonzalez (the Pampas Bull) raced his Ferrari 375 to victory over an Alfa Romeo 158. In 1952 the great Alberto Ascari won Ferrari's first world title.

These were the passions which Pininfarina needed to illustrate in its extraordinary series of road cars for Ferrari. Eventually, they became the greatest cars of them all. Enzo Ferrari was interested only in motor-racing (my terrible joys, as he described it) and only made road cars as a concession to business practicalities and also because his racing customers demanded them. Ferrari, almost reluctantly, chose to collaborate with Pininfarina. Rarely, if ever, can such condescension have created such ravishing beauty.

The Pininfarina collaboration began with the 212 Inter, a small coupé with a 2562cc V12 engine produced in greater numbers than any of its predecessors. Earlier versions of the 212 had been clothed in bodywork by various of the Italian *carrozzerie*, including Vignale and Touring, but Pininfarina was able to capture the essence of the Ferrari idea. Ferrari may have been primarily interested in racing cars, but even his uncompromisingly functional *monoposti* – the 375 F1 of 1951, for example – were distinguished by a magnificent handsomeness which cannot have been accidental.

Perhaps it was a meeting of minds, or, at least, egos that made the Farina and Ferrari collaboration so fecund. When it was decided to do

business, each was so proud that the one refused to travel to Modena, the other refused to travel to Turin. Instead, they met on neutral ground (it is said) at the Hostaria ai Due Gioghi at Tortona, 70km (44 miles) from Genoa. Pinin drove there in his own Lancia Aurelia B20. There is no record of the conversation, but the Lancia was an effective advertisment and ever since Pininfarina has created the image of Ferrari... *alla maniera di Pininfarina*.

But Pinin continued to work for a wide range of other clients too, initially in Italy alone, but eventually throughout Europe. His 1954 Lancia Aurelia B24 roadster – a more artistically developed and more conversationally subtle Nash-Healey – brought the formal language he had developed for Ferrari to a larger public. But it was Pininfarina's great rival, Bertone, which was the first *carrozzeria* to design a real mass-market GT. This was Bertone's Alfa Romeo Giulietta, a compact, restrained, but supremely elegant little coupé.

But then, as if the aristocratic Pininfarina and Bertone were in competition for influence in the fast-evolving European motor-trade, in 1955 Pininfarina entered into a contract with Peugeot. It would be inelegant, perhaps, to describe Peugeot (also known as a bicycle manufacturer) as proletarian, but the alliance with Pininfarina extended the reach of Italian design beyond the exclusive Ferrari and the specialists Lancia and Alfa Romeo. Ever since, Peugeot has used Pininfarina as a design consultant.

Then in 1957 Pinin made a very bold move. Instead of proposing new designs on customer chassis, at the Torino Salone of that year he showed a car that, while based on Lancia running gear, was not identified with any make, but presented as something magnificent in its own right. This was the Florida II, one of the most significant cars never to have gone into production. It was a unique design: bold, undecorated sides, big airy glasshouse, elegant proportions. It was the automobile equivalent of a Brioni suit and set an aesthetic standard for European passenger cars that lasted for 30 years. That year, 1957, was when all the assumptions about car design established in the preceding half-century were at last forgotten. If in Pininfarina's Lancia B24 it is possible to see the faintest ghosts of a Thirties sports car, the Florida II was entirely uncontaminated by heritage.

Influence spread even, yea, unto Longbridge and Cowley, industrial homes of the British Motor Corporation. Since the arrival of Riccardo Burzi in Longbridge from Lancia in Turin in the early Fifties, there had been some covert Italian influence at Austin (his cute Austin A35 has, if you adjust your sight and abandon prejudices, something of an Italianate feel), but the influence of Pininfarina became explicit when Leonard Lord of BMC signed the maestro. This was not Lord's first encounter with the human exotica of design consultancy: he had also engaged the fabulous Raymond Loewy, but the relationship was never consummated with a vehicle. Loewy told the story about making a presentation in Birmingham, revealing his proposals with the glorious legerdemain of a charlatan-genius. There was muted, polite approval from the grim Midlands businessmen who were his

Reachunder, adjustwasher, screwdown bolt, shove in cotter pin, reachunder, adjustwasher, screwdown bolt, reachunderadjustscrewdownreachunderadjust

John Dos Passos, *U.S.A.: The Big Money*, 1933

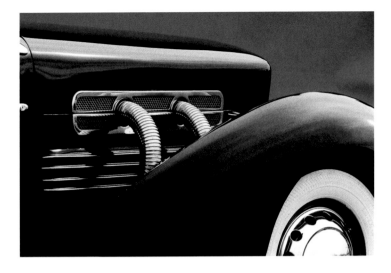

audience. But nothing was implemented. Loewy called Lord long distance to ask why. 'Goodness me, Mr Loewy!' the reply went. 'We never intended to use your designs. We were simply interested to see what you were thinking.'

Alas, there are no detailed accounts of the meeting between Pininfarina and Leonard Lord, although photographs exist showing a slightly baffled Torinese sophisticate shaking hands in Brum gloom. This engagement led to more fruitful stuff than Loewy's. Soon Pininfarina sketched the Austin A40, the world's first hatchback. And the Morris Oxford shows a fine consanguinity with the contemporary Peugeot 404. This is, depending on your point of view, either perfect evidence of Pininfarina's confident aesthetic or cynical exploitation of credulous manufacturers, selling the same set of drawings twice. Still, it is wonderful to know that a 1960 Morris Oxford has something in common with a 1951 Ferrari 212 Inter.

The Pininfarina technique was singular. While in Detroit cars were designed by executive committees responding to marketing plans, features lists and the adjustments required by fixed-cost accountants, in Turin the processes were much more artisanal and in direct contact with workshop practices of the Middle Ages and Renaissance. From the most extemporary sketches by the master, a draughtsman would prepared technical drawings. Then a wooden buck would be made. This would be criticized and adjusted. Sometimes the finished item would be modified, or even destroyed, with a hammer. Or more properly, a martello. Well into the Seventies designers and craftsmen at Pininfarina's automated facility at Grugliasco were still using Piedmontese dialect to describe the handtools they employed: *cantines, baquet, bicorna, strompor, ciav a papagal* are all terms that survive in Pininfarina's Lessico della Carrozzeria.

But even when they spoke the more correct Italian of Dante, Pinin and the other Italian design entrepreneurs had access to a vocabulary unknown in other languages. An Italian designer can talk about *montante* or *nervatura*

or a *figurino*, a *sguscio* and the *campanatura*. As philosophers of language know, if you have a word for something, chances are you will be able to give it more attention. In Italy there is a term to describe the area and the angle where a car's windscreen meets its bonnet. Inevitably, if you have a word to describe such a thing (and none exists in English) you are more likely to pay special attention to its concept and execution. It is this level of sophistication in language that, among many other positively stimulating attributes belonging to a culture where Michelangelo is a council household name, has made Italian car design so beautiful and so influential.

The successor to Pininfarina and Bertone is Giorgetto Giugiaro. He was born in 1938 and studied at the Belli Arti in Turin, leaving for FIAT when he was 17. At 21 he joined Nuccio Bertone and in 1965 he became chief executive of the design centre of Ghia. He set up his own firm, ItalDesign, in 1968. While still with Bertone he designed the Alfa Romeo Giulia GT, a car widely considered to be one of the understated classics of all time. At ItalDesign Giugiaro's esoteric influence was huge before he became known as a cult figure. ItalDesign worked on the Alfa Romeo Alfasud (1971), on the Volkswagen Golf (1974) and on the FIAT Panda (1980). The first stage of the presentation included two full-scale models, four alternative solutions for the sides, a back of the passenger compartment and a comprehensive comparative study putting the Panda-to-be alongside its competitors. When these proposals were approved, ItalDesign was requested to start production studies, build a master model and design provisional tooling and engineer pre-production prototypes. Within a year, ItalDesign had produced 20 rolling chassis.

The oil crisis of 1973 stimulated a change in Giugiaro's views about design. Having established a particular mode of stylish sporting car – extreme, angular, mid-engined designs for de Tomaso, Maserati and Lotus – he changed to a more practical, more functional one. He even

I think that cars today are almost the exact equivalent of the great Gothic cathedrals: I mean the supreme creation of an era, conceived with passion by unknown artists, and consumed in an image if not in usage by a whole population which appropriates them as a purely magical object.

Roland Barthes, *Mythologies*, 1957

began to practise a form of obsolescence, saying, 'I contributed to making the long, low, sleek car fashionable, and now it is time to change. I have to eat, you know.'

Since the firm has become recognized as *the* leading Italian car design consultancy, more and more effort has gone into producing speculative dream cars, unveiled to the industry of the world at every year's Turin Motor Show. Giugiaro designs sewing-machines for Necchi, cameras for Nikon, watches for Seiko, crash-helmets for Shoiei and furniture for Tecno. While his car designs all share a crisp, razor-edged elegance, Giugiaro's product designs can be recognized by a deliberately 'technical' aesthetic. Somewhat bitchily, Uwe Bahnsen, the Ford designer responsible for the Sierra, described Giugiaro's style as 'origami' and added, 'I think he is stretching himself what with pasta and trousers and cameras.' What is certain is that Giugiaro stretched the language of European car design.

One of the first cars to carry his autograph was the 1966 de Tomaso Mangusta, a product of no industrial, technological or commercial significance, but a magnificent example of his handwriting. 'Pretty enough to make you weep,' according to Rich Taylor in 1978 who explained, 'There wasn't any part you could single out and say, "There, that's what makes it so beautiful" [but] the surface tension in the bodywork was so precise, so effortless, you got the feeling there was no other possible shape that would fit that space. It was, to be sure, an art object. But more, it was an organic, growing, living thing that changed as you walked around it, that made your hear beat faster as you looked at it. Giugiaro's Mangusta was "towards a natural automobile" the way Frank Lloyd Wright's Taliesin was "toward a natural architecture". Giugiaro handled plastic volumes better than any Italian since Michelangelo.'

In Britain there was another source of Italian influence, significant not in terms of the mass market, but of the mass-appeal created by aggregates of favourable imagery. The Sean Connery iteration of James Bond drove an Aston-Martin, a car that is apparently the quintessence of Englishness (although Ian Fleming's spy drove a Bentley in literature). However, the beautiful bodies of the DB4 and DB5 were designed and made to patented *superleggera* principles by Carrozzeria Touring of Milan. It is true that this *carrozzeria* (founded in 1926) was in its choice of Anglophone name acknowledging a cultural debt to old English ideas of elegance associated with the Grand Tour, but it is instructive how the essence of national characteristics – the handsome toughness of the Aston, its well-mannered, but indomitable aspect – can be captured by alien forces. In the same way, Connery-Bond's exquisite suits were, in fact, made by Brioni of Rome.

An indigenous native English tradition in car design had three different sources. There was the magnificent country house architecture of John Blatchley in his masterpieces for Bentley and Rolls-Royce (not, in either case, it must be admitted, wholly without influence from Italy and America, via Pininfarina and Harley Earl: Blatchley's best have fastbacks and fins). Then there was the school of inspired (if financially ruinous) ingenuity and inventiveness which found expression in the exquisite Lotus Elite and austere Mini. Finally, there was the low taste for Americana, perhaps the most influential taste of all.

It was Americana that gave us the Ford Cortina, which, depending on your methodologies, might be considered the most successful of British cars. In terms of technology it was conservative, possibly even backward, but in terms of consumer psychology it was consummate: the Cortina delivered a digestible portion of Americana to a population for whom rationing and gas masks were a recent memory. The Cortina's designer was Roy A. Brown, whose violent career dips did not compromise his feelings of self-worth: 'I have so much talent, it frightens me,' he once said.

Brown's biggest career dip, a Marianas Trench of a dip, was the 1958

Opposite left: One time racing driver Errett Lobban Cord designed and manufactured superlatively sculptural automobiles in very small numbers. This is the Cord 812, 1937. The Cord Corporation did not survive the Second World War, but Cord himself became one of the first owners of Californian television stations.

Opposite right: The great photographer Jacques-Henri Lartigue often used cars as meaningful props in his images of the good life. This is 'Renee en route' (between Paris and Aix-les-Bains), 1931.

Above left: With their ponderous handling, great weight and weak brakes, American cars of the Fifties were often better suited to the drive-in than to driving. Pierre Belzeaux's photograph captures the spirit of a consumer culture in thrall to the automobile.

Above right: A BMW 328 with special bodywork for the Mille Miglia road race, 1940. In the background, designer Wilhelm Meyerhuber, who had trained under Harley Earl at General Motors in Detroit. The 328 MM influenced the more famous Jaguar XK120.

Ford Edsel, a car market-researched and product-planned with such pitiless commitment that its total failure left Ford's management bewildered. And, indeed, demoralized and embarrassed, since it was construed as a vanity project. Brown had photographed and studied every contemporary Detroit nose treatment and became determined to avoid the oppressive horizontality that was the design norm. So, in search of what American advertisement executive Rosser Reeves was soon to call a 'unique selling proposition', Brown gave the Edsel a vertical grille, rather like a chromed horse's collar. Had the car been produced in significant enough numbers, customers would have discovered that this wilful gesture would have had practical limitations since it did not allow enough cooling air for the Edsel's voracious engine. But the Edsel was a colossal flop: there was some speculation that the shape of grille excited unconscious notions of the vagina, which many found unsettling.

But the career of Roy A. Brown is certain proof of the caprice of consumer behaviour and the almost complete lack of science, or even mere rationality, in car design. After the calamitous Edsel, Brown was exiled to Ford's Dagenham gulag. In this creative Siberia he drew the epochal Cortina. That same Edsel may have failed because of occult erotic morphology. Yet another successful British car won great esteem because of explicit erotic morphology. This was the gorgeous and raffish Jaguar

E-Type, the near contemporary of the lower-middle-class Cortina. In Jaguar all the elements of British car design came together: a Spitfire-spirit sense of inspired ingenuity; a taste for wood, leather and carpet directly attributable to the national preoccupation with visiting country houses; plus a knowing, even sly, commercialism inspired by America.

But sex, or a version of it, was the most significant factor in the E-Type's celebrity. The design is attributed to Jaguar's proprietor, Sir William Lyons, and his brown-coated aerodynamicist, Malcolm Sayer. The process was intuitive. Clearly, significant formal elements were carried over from Jaguar's successful Le Mans sports-racing cars, but equally clearly, the whole was much more than the sum of inherited parts. There is no documentary record of the Lyons–Sayer collaboration, but whatever processes they employed resulted in a novel synthesis: a design founded in precedent, but achieving something wholly original. It seems doubtful that Lyons and Sayer were consciously in pursuit of sexual expressionism, although that is what was achieved. The E-Type's shape, proportions and detail are unambiguously phallic. As Havelock Ellis explained in *Studies in the Psychology of Sex* (1906), 'The exhibitionist is not usually content to produce a mere titillated amusement; he seeks to produce a more powerful effect which must be emotional whether or not it is pleasurable.'

Thus the famous and exhibitionist E-Type became the first mass-produced car to be on permanent display in New York's Museum of Modern Art (the first two cars in this shrine of educated taste were the Cisitalia and a Grand Prix Ferrari). It was the Museum of Modern Art that inaugurated the serious study of car design when in 1951 Arthur Drexler curated an exhibition called 'Eight Automobiles'. Some were bespoke craftsmanship, others mass-produced. They were the '30 Mercedes-Benz SS, '37 Cord, '39 Bentley Mark VI, '39 Figoni & Falaschi Talbot, '41 Lincoln Continental, '48 MG TC, '49 Cisitalia and '51 Jeep. Drexler said they were 'rolling sculpture'. His account of the Cisitalia is a masterpiece of formal analysis:

'[Its] body is slipped over its chassis like a dustjacket over a book… the openings Farina cuts into the jacket provide some of the most skillfully contrived details of automotive design… to maintain the sculptural unity of the entire shape, its surfaces are never joined with sharp edges, but are instead wrapped around and blunted. The door is minimized. The back of the car, particularly the fender, is lifted at an angle rising from the strict horizontal baseline which gives stability to the design. Thus, both ends of the car gain an extraordinary tension, as though its metal skin did not quite fit over the framework and had to be stretched into place. This accounts, in part, for that quality of animation which makes the Cisitalia seem larger than it is.'

But the acceptance of car design as an important aspect of contemporary culture had its equivalent in a mounting critique of the automobile as a

The automobile manufacturers have made, in the past few years, a greater contribution to the art of comfortable seating than chair builders in all preceding history.

Walter Dorwin Teague, 1940.

We value speed more highly than we value human life.

George Orwell, 1946

dangerous, polluting instrument of social division. Vance Packard's *The Wastemakers* (1960) mocked consumerism. Ralph Nader's *Unsafe at Any Speed*, a damagingly critical account of the Chevrolet Corvair's lack of roadworthiness, announced in the early Sixties the beginning of the end of American domination of the global auto industry. Not immediately, but eventually and irrevocably, Nader's account of General Motors' corporate negligence fatally undermined the confidence of one of the world's mightiest manufacturers.

In his review of Nader, the social critic Lewis Mumford (who had been so curmudgeonly about the glorious Chrysler Building) renewed his assault on what was still America's premier product. The American car, he wrote, 'has been the result of a secret collaboration between the beautician and the mortician; and according to sales and accident statistics, both have reason to be satisfied'. In the year of the Oldsmobile Toronado, General Motors' last great *tour de force*, Ralph Nader made American cars appear both dangerous and ridiculous. Designers had made them look astonishing, but far from keeping slightly in front of consumer taste, Detroit completely failed to anticipate an age of new values. After the Sixties, there was never another great American car.

Now car designers work in a very different cultural environment: industrially, it is all more competitive; socially, less sympathetic; environmentally, much more critical. While once competitive advantage might be won with whimsy and pearlescent paint, an ever more highly educated consumer is far less susceptible to the blandishments of mere novelty.

One hundred years after Ford's 'First Car', technological distinctions between competing vehicles have been to a very substantial degree eroded: while once there were good, bad and indifferent, even dangerous, cars, today the machinery all works well. Legislation requires it. Even if today anyone thought it sane to do a '59 Cadillac, Health and Safety would not allow it. Nor, of course, would the environmental lobby. Rather, as Lord Chesterfield said of sex, the pleasure is momentary, the position ridiculous, the expense damnable. But ferocious competition and stifling legislation have not produced banality in car design – they have encouraged ever greater sophistication. The car buyer is a consumer who understands a marvellously sophisticated language of nuances and gestures. Discussions of symbolic form which once might have merited inclusion in the post graduate programme at Columbia University's Institute of Fine Art have become mundane for the car buyer.

Consumer choice, at least in the West and Japan, is rarely based wholly on functional, let alone rational, considerations. Instead, consumers choose on the basis of social competition and cultural modelling. Accordingly, the

Opposite: Although military intelligence is an oxymoron, the Jeep was designed to a demanding and stimulating US Army brief. The result is an enduring design classic: uncompromisingly simple, as a graphic composition the Jeep cannot be improved. Shown here during the Detroit race riots of June, 1943.

Above: The Pininfarina-designed Cisitalia defined the shape of the post-War Grand Touring car. So pure, simple and structural, it was the first car acquired for the permanent design collection of New York's Museum of Modern Art.

competitive areas in the motor industry are now imagery and symbolism, the absolute substance of art. J. Mays, chief creative officer of Ford, says, 'It's easy to design a part; the difficult thing is to tell a story.' While once 'design' was an industrial option, now it is a commercial imperative.

The car designer's task has evolved in much the same way as the automobile itself. He has to travel, creatively speaking, to the very end of the alphabet. And he needs to do more than simply play with letters of the alphabet, he needs to construct literate stories. When it is recognized in the market place that the name 'Porsche' is worth more than all the factories, patents and other assets Porsche owns, then understanding and communicating the meaning of that name becomes a paramount business necessity. This has become the car designer's responsibility.

So you hear as much about DNA in car design studios as in genetics laboratories: every one is concerned to understand how a design transmits meaning across the generations. Everyone is concerned to capture the essence of a brand. It is exactly as Gilbert Simondon wrote in *Du mode d'existence des objets techniques* (1958):

> *'Artifacts evolve using themselves as the point of departure: they contain the conditions for their own development. The structure of the object moves to match the future conditions in which it will be employed.'*

So with great art, successive Porsches look similar to, but different from, their predecessors. It as the old man said in Lampedusa's *The Leopard* (1958): if you want things to stay the same, they are going to have to change. Significantly, the current chief designer at Porsche is English. In Harley Earl's day a Chevrolet was an American responsibility. But international markets and distributed intelligence have made car design international, sometimes almost surrealistically so. The BMW 5-series launched, to some controversy, in 2003 was designed by an American, Chris Bangle (who used to work for FIAT in Turin). The Rolls-Royce 100EX concept car – a road-going adaptation of an English gentleman's yacht – was designed by Marek Djordevic. And the designer responsible for Skoda's renaissance in the 1990s, a Belgian called Dirk von Braeckl, was promoted to aristocratic Bentley. Here van Braeckl has created a new Continental, using an entirely original visual language which, with great finesse, evokes the country house architecture that Bentley's hero-designer, John Blatchley, applied to his masterpiece, the 1952 Bentley Continental 'R'. To add another dimension still, Bentley is now owned by Volkswagen, manufacturer of the people's car. Clearly, this DNA got lost en route.

Despite their global markets, car designers tend to live in a hermetic world, meeting their peers in airline first-class lounges more often than they meet their customers on the street. Often, their sources of inspiration are bizarre. The Italians were in a quest for a technologically pure *bella figura*:

'Il peso e il nemico e la resistenza d'aria l'ostocolo'. Weight is the enemy and wind resistance the obstacle, according to Felice Bianchi Anderloni and Gaetano Ponzoni. Anderloni was almost certainly the author of the original Ferrari: the 166 Barchetta, or little boat. More recently, Pinky Lai, while working in the Porsche studios, cited the Hong Kong Star Ferry, the music of Pat Metheny and trainers as his inspiration. Land Rover's Gerry McGovern has cited women's Lycra-clad bottoms. Others cite guns and Fender Stratocasters as inspiration. Most designers have a model Ferrari somewhere in their office, although van Braeckl's successor at Skoda, a German called Thomas Ingenlath, has mood boards in his studio encouraging imitation of IKEA's no-nonsense functionalism.

Sources are eclectic, results mixed, but one thing is certain: car design is being forced up an ever tightening helix of creativity. Car design has usurped the roles contemporary art has abandoned: the public learns about symbolism, form, about how light falls on objects, how details can articulate meaning from cars… not from the avant-garde. Put it this way: if two machines framed American experience, one would be the Model T with no bodywork, the other would be Kennedy's SS-100-X with special bodywork by Hess & Eisenhardt of Cincinnati.

It seems poetic that one of America's greatest cars is for ever associated with one of America's greatest tragedies, but if Eros is an influence on car design, Thanatos has a role, too. Many great artists caught the poignancy of cars whose promise of freedom and mobility so often mocks the precarious predicament of most of us. Grant Wood's painting *Death on Ridge Road* (Smithsonian, Washington,1935) shows a collision on a country road, the dark side of the American Dream. *Joe's Auto Graveyard*, one of Walker Evans' pictures taken of cars for the Farm Securities Administration in 1933, shows an even darker one. James Dean helped secure Porsche's reputation through his well-publicized fatal collision with Donald Turnipseed's Ford truck. The incongruity of the vehicles involved in the incident, Dean's screaming Porsche racer and the plebian Ford, seems significant. Dean had the legend 'Little Bastard' painted on his Porsche's tail. Albert Camus ('action-packed intellectual' according to *Life* magazine) hated driving fast, but died when his publisher, Michel Gallimard, lost control of his Facel-Vega HK500 on the RN5 south of Paris. It was 3 January 1960. On such matters are literary and design reputations defined. The sales department might be reluctant to acknowledge it, but psycho-pathology, sexualization and death are all involved in car design, as J.G. Ballard explained in 'The Atrocity Exhibition' in *Love and Napalm* (1969). In 1973 Ballard's distinctly dystopian novel *Crash* (later turned into a movie by David Cronenberg) fetishized the erotic nature of automobile trauma.

While verbal language is rarely their strength, car designers have occasionally made curious contributions to the development of English. While involved in his surreal aesthetic adventures in the mid-Fifties,

Nature builds no machines.

Karl Marx, 1848

I want that line to have a duflunky, to come across, have a little hook in it, and then do a rashoom or a zong.

Harley Earl, mid 1950s

Harley Earl found the limitations of Shakespeare's English too inhibiting (just as he had said 'mere artistry is limiting'). So as English failed to keep pace with Earl's inventiveness, he had to mint his own coinage to express the baroque oddness of his design ideas. One day in the spooky sci-fi modern GM Tech Center at Warren, Michigan, Earl (very possibly wearing a cinnamon-coloured linen suit and high-shine wingtip loafers) explained to an audience of acolytes, at once impressed and mystified that:

'I want that line to have a duflunky, to come across, have a little hook in it, and then do a rashoom or a zong.'

Then there is the question of onomastics, or the naming of the parts. A famous episode that defines the industry's approach to English while at its baroque peak involved the Edsel. Vox-pop research took place at Willow Run Airport, chosen because the travellers were reliably well-off. Simultaneously, the agency Foote, Cone and Belding ran competitions in its New York, Chicago and London offices. Eighteen thousand entries were received. They got it down to 6,000 for a presentation, a level of complexity that displeased Ford staff who had inherited Henry's spirit of economy. They wanted ten.

So they thought instead about a poet. Robert Frost was considered because he was one of those men with 'a real feel for words that pull', although no one commented that his preference for being an outsider (*The Road Not Taken*, 1916, where he says, 'I took the one less traveled by') might have disqualified him from the mass market. Marianne Moore was chosen instead, not least because she had written enthusiastically about the Dodgers, suggestive of populist sensibilities. She refused an upfront fee because 'My fancy would be inhibited… by acknowledgement in advance of performance.'

Uninhibited, her fancy suggested in a letter Thunderblender, the Reslient Bullet, the Ford Fabergé, the Intelligent Whale, the Mongoose Civique, the Pastelogram, the Varsity Stroke, Andante con Moto, Turcotinga and Utopian Turtletop (among many others). 'Do not,' the poetess wrote to the bewildered Ford executive, 'trouble to answer unless you like it.' The whole process having been santized with PR gloss, was, eventually published in the *New Yorker*. And US industry's greatest stinker was left as the Edsel, not, alas, the Utopian Turtletop.

The car industry requires designers to work to extraordinary disciplines. Someone will know how to remove a few euros of manufacturing costs

Above: Walker Evans, Joe's Auto Graveyard, 1933. Any car's transit from gleaming desirability to rotting and rusting desuetude is a metaphor of life itself.

from a particular moulding. It is not all heroic acts of autonomous creativity: whole careers can be spent achieving little. Circa 1970 at Ford's English design facility at Dunton, Essex, it took 5.7 man months for designers and 9.3 man months for modellers to produce six steering-wheel designs for the Mark III Cortina. It was not even a particularly good steering wheel.

The American corporations have lost their influence. General Motors was conceived and grew in a culture where Richard Buckminster Fuller could, in 1940, insist that God was a verb, not a noun. General Motors gave the world the model of a gargantuan corporation with all its parallel divisions, hierarchies, global reach, management science, McKinseyite principles. It stimulated Peter Drucker's management classic *The Concept of the Corporation* (1946) and Alfred Sloan's autobiographical *My Years at General Motors* (1964). Sloan had found a ragbag of provincial engineering firms working on cars and fridges and everything in between and amalgamated them into 'a growth company'.

The great adventure of mass-market car design began when Sloan was brought in to support brand separation. For rather a long time, it was a majestic construct. Never mind the cars, in the Forties and Fifties General Motors dominated the American consumer's conception of how life might be. Between 1947 and 1955 the American Dream was expressed in the American kitchen. The roster of GM's new products in that eight-year stretch runs: homefood freezers, automatic washers, dryers, automatic ice-cube makers, dishwashers, wall ovens. Now the most impressive sight in the General Motors universe is a robot-populated facility in Slovakia, manufacturing cars made by its Korean subsidiary, Kia. They are as blandly efficient as kitchen equipment.

E. B. White anticipated the end rather sooner. Although in *Farewell to Model T* he described the Ford as a 'miracle that God had wrought', in 1936 'The great days have faded, the end is in sight.' There followed a long, slow, elegiac descent to the delirium of suburban anomie suggested in Robert Bechtle's hyper-realist paintings. One such shows a stultified family with their '61 Pontiac. Not for nothing did Bechtle become known as the 'poet of the parking lot'. Beyond his stultified subject, to adapt Lewis Mumford's words, lies only another suburb, just as dull as his own.

But if the car helped to destroy destinations, the car also became a destination in its own right, not merely a means of connection. In a 1955 article in *Industrial Design* magazine, the journalist Eric Larrabee caught the mood:

'Stand at night, on a corner in a strange town, and watch the cars go by. What is there so poignant in this? A sense of private destinies, of each making his own choice, of being independent of everything but statistics. The cars' owners choose – or think they do – when to stop and start, where to go. The automobile offers a vista of escape: for the adolescent from parental planning; for the Negro, from Jim Crow; and for others, from less formal restrictions on their freedom of movement. Thus they are liberated to the loneliness (and perplexity) of their independence, and thus travel on the highway at night acquires its own tones of adventure and sorrow.'

When the facts change, I change my mind, or so the economist J. M. Keynes once said. Fifty years after Larrabee, there have been many changes – political, economic, artistic, technological, environmental – but dreams of escape remain a part of any car's appeal. As late as 1992, a year after Gulf War Mark One, advertising copy for the *Mercury Sable* could indulge in perfumed romanticism (with an erotic edge obvious perhaps only to late Freudians). To support an unremarkable Ford product, a copywriter describes a journey from town to country, a journey drenched with symbolism: 'We dressed in silence. And drove. Until four lanes became two. Two became one. And one became a tunnel… something that was there before was back.'

Of course, from the perspective of the twenty-first century it seems very clear that some things are never coming back, the '59 Cadillac being one example. The 1955 Citroën DS and 1963 Ferrari 250 GTO being others. Nor, perhaps, will there ever again be such a conceptual revolution as the one that produced the 1959 Mini. The great age of car design is over or, at least, its assumptions have changed.

Cadillac is bereft, Citroën imports Japanese cars and badges them with André Citroën's idiosyncratic chevrons, Ferrari has become a vulgarian parody of itself, a travesty of the purist principles which inspired its creation. The most significant car of recent years has been the modest smart. An inheritor of the culture of Germany's Kleinwagen, the bubble cars of the Wirtschaftswunder where native engineering genius adapted to regimes of severe restraint, the slow and tiny smart is an ingenious new format that changed the consumer's expectations and enhanced their potential as much as the Mini did 40 years before.

The design criteria for the smart included packaging efficiency, fuel economy and low impact on space and resources generally. So it has very little in common with, say, a Chevrolet Corvette. Except it shares certain basic assumptions about what a car should be: a private, mobile, controlled environment exisiting for the pleasure and convenience of the owner. Hence the Nissan Cube, a car with conventions of beauty left far behind it, but significant because it finally blurs a distinction, a long time eroding, between product design and car styling. It has more in common with an iPod than a Maserati.

Henry Ford's 'faster horses' have had their run. Since, a century of glorious inventiveness when 'freedom, style, sex, power, motion, colour' and everything else which excites consumers took refuge in the car. Freedom seems a delusion, the rest a selfish indulgence. But magnificent, nonetheless.

Some say the world will end in fire, Some say in ice.

Robert Frost, 'Fire and Ice', 1923.

1908

Ford Model T

'Faster horses' was Henry Ford's rationale of the car. He was not the designer of the Model T (that was the work of his close friend Childe Harold Willis, assisted by two Hungarian émigrés, Josef Galamb and Eugene Farkas), but it was an expression of his genius. This was the car that motorized America, its driver becoming, in the author E. B. White's words 'a man enthroned'. Ford's famous production lines were inspired by a visit to a Chicago slaughterhouse. By 1914 it took Ford only 93 minutes to assemble a car. The achievement excited Aldous Huxley into a delirious admiration for speed. In his futuristic classic, *Brave New World*, Huxley started measuring the calendar in 'Years of Our Ford'. White described the planetary gearbox as 'half metaphysics, half friction'. The innovations were neither technological nor aesthetic, but social and commercial. The car democratized the luxury of travel; not so much an influence on the American scene as the American scene itself. The Model T's development was the US system in miniature: as sales rose, prices dropped. The first Model Ts were dark blue, but when Henry Ford discovered that black paint dried more quickly, you could have one in any colour so long as it was black. (With daily production taking up about 20 acres, this economy brought immediate cost benefits.) Tough vanadium steel and simple components made it indestructible. There were electric starters by 1919. By the Twenties, prices had fallen to less than $300. At one point in the car's 19-year life, more pages of the Sears Roebuck catalogue were devoted to Model T spare parts than to men's clothing. As late as 1936, you could still have a rear axle sent through the post. At a dinner celebrating the millionth Model T, Henry Ford stood up and simply said, 'Gentlemen, a million of anything is a great many.'

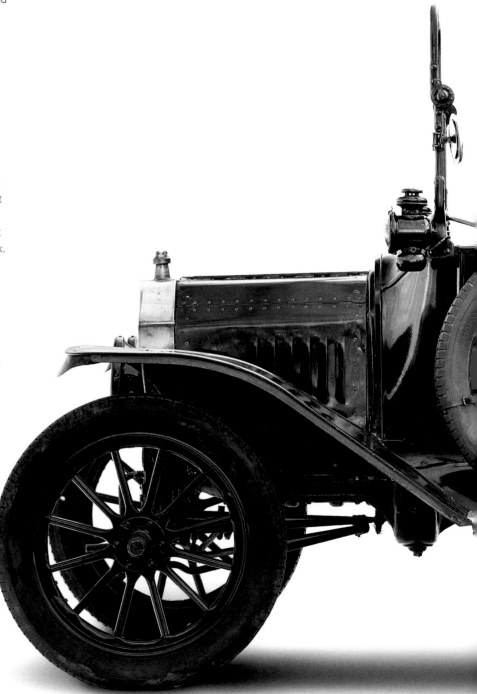

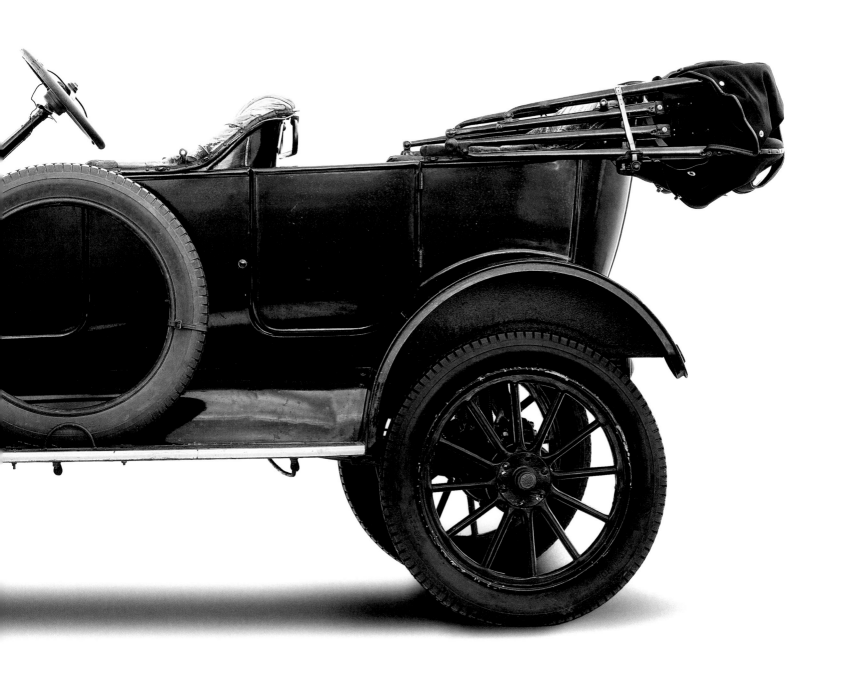

1934

Citroën 11CV Traction Avant

André Citroën was influenced by Ford and by US automated construction techniques. Indeed, with his taste for publicity and his astute understanding of his countrymen's psychology, Citroën could be said to be the French Ford. This car is his Model T, though being French it was more luxurious. From the start, visionary procedures were involved. Safety was an innovation: the first crash test had the car pushed off a cliff. There was front-wheel drive, a rigid body, independent front suspension. The body was drawn by Flaminio Bertoni, an Italian sculptor with connections to the Futurists and Surrealists. It is said that, using a sculptor's tools, Bertoni designed the body in the course of a single night in his atelier at Citroën's Bureau des Etudes. The Traction Avant was dramatically lower than its

contemporaries: front-wheel drive allowed the placing of the passenger cell between the wheels and closer to the ground. Because of André Citroën's belief that 'dès l'instant qu'une idée est bonne, le prix n'a pas d'importance' costs were, however, high and led to bankruptcy. Still, Citroën's chief engineer, André Lefebvre, was able to exploit his employer's generous brief. Lefebvre had worked for the Voisin company, manufacturer of aircraft and cars, that was the darling and inspiration of architect Le Corbusier. To celebrate his company's place in French life, André Citroën built a Champs-Elysées showroom more like a museum than a garage. He ran his name in lights up the Eiffel Tower. Under Michelin ownership 800,000 Traction Avants were produced before production ended in 1957.

1935

Lincoln Zephyr

Lincoln was Ford's premium brand and the Zephyr was its mass-market offer, a route for the consumer from the most expensive Fords to the premier Lincoln line. It was a conceit of Henry Ford's son, Edsel, the first American to acquire an English MG sports car. The cable-operated brakes on the Zephyr were *retardataire*, but its light, rigid, monocoque body was radical. The designer was Tom Tjaarda, who had made boat-tailed speedster personal cars for Edsel. The Zephyr name was a deliberate reference to the Burlington Silver Streak Zephyr, a steam locomotive of great romance exhibited at the 1934 Chicago 'Century of Progress' exhibition where Tjaarda's first thoughts on the Zephyr appeared as a concept car. While his father was obdurately utilitarian, Edsel had a taste for flash. The Zephyr acquired a radical shape that sloped and tapered unfashionably. With it Tjaarda grasped the slippery semantics of streamlining more

successfully than the famous Chrysler Airflow or the long-forgotten Hupp Aerodynamic by Raymond Loewy. His design was refined by Eugene Turenne 'Bob' Gregorie, hitherto a yacht designer for Cox & Stevens in New York. Indeed, the Zephyr has a nose like an inverted ship's bow. With 15,000 manufactured in 1936, the Zephyr was one of the very first attempts by a mass-market manufacturer to consumerize all available ideas of luxury and style: it was conceived as an integrated, elegant, compact, subtle whole, painted in delicious colours. Gregorie's design received a US patent and was described by the Museum of Modern Art as the first successful American streamlined car. While the production stopped on 31 January 1942, the Zephyr DNA was passed on to the larger 1941 Lincoln Continental and ultimately, to the '61 Continental, the most gorgeous of all American cars.

1936

Chrysler Airflow

In the Chrysler Airflow, engineer Carl Breer brought together Art Deco and streamlining in a car. Inspired by the sight of geese flying in a V-formation, and also by the Burlington Zephyr, it became the chosen car of New York mayor Fiorello LaGuardia. Walter Chrysler – a one-time mechanic for Union Pacific Railroad – had a reputation for radical engineering, at least by conservative American standards. The Airflow benefited from pioneering use of a wind tunnel, brought about when an intermediary contacted flight pioneer Orville Wright. It was soon determined that conventional cars of the era were more aerodynamically efficient when travelling backwards. Breer's architecture placed passengers within the wheelbase, to achieve even weight distribution. Walter Chrysler, a friend of impresario Flo Ziegfeld, approved the research and enjoyed the attendant hullabaloo. And, for the first time, the engine was moved forward of the front wheel centre-line. This new geometry allowed a new architecture: influential, wonderful, but commercially ruinous (even if an ingenious economy included the

interchangeability of right-front and left-rear doors). The Airflow offered exceptional internal space in an envelope of unusual integrity, but the public was not enthusiastic, despite endorsement from celebrity designer Norman Bel Geddes. The Airflow was simplified, then abandoned in 1937, although it remained in production long enough to have been a possible influence on Porsche's Volkswagen. Indisputably, the first Toyota was virtually a copy. A 1934 advertisement in *Fortune* said, 'By scientific experiment, Chrysler engineers have simply verified and adapted a natural fundamental law,' but when Orville Wright actually tested the Airflow in a wind tunnel its aerodynamic performance was no better than average.

1939

BMW 328 Mille Miglia

Kurt Joachimson's 1936 BMW 328 was the first modern sports car: fast, safe and reliable, with design that expressed that originality. It had faired-in headlights, cutaway doors, a sense of spareness. Dash and logic are dominant motifs, but the essential simplicity is, in fact, a hard-won subtlety. *Autocar*'s road test of 16 July 1937 concluded 'It is difficult to think of this machine in terms that apply to the more ordinary type of car… Very nearly unique…' The streamlined competition version was drawn by BMW's Wilhelm Meyerhuber in the company's pioneering department of Künstlerische Gestaltung, or artistic development. The shape is both scientifically aerodynamic and lasciviously beautiful; restrained, yet flamboyantly seductive. No details intrude upon a perfectly conceived whole. A small handful were made by Carrozzeria Touring of Milan. The 328 Mille Miglia, a unique expression of German genius, was a clear influence on the postwar English Jaguar XK120. After the Second World War, the British Frazer-Nash company of Isleworth acquired production rights as part of war reparations. 'British' Frazer-Nash-BMWs featured distinctive ventilated steel wheels. The British contribution was having the holes drilled in Middlesex. The British think of themselves as sports car pioneers, but the origin of the modern sports car was German.

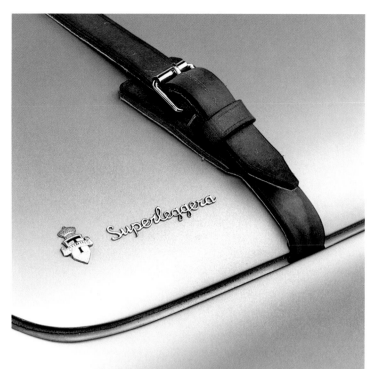

1941

Jeep

The predecessor of the famous Jeep was a stripped-down, weaponized Ford Model T. The US Government made a call for proposals – an RFB or 'Request for Bid' – from American Bantam, Ford and Willys-Overland, allowing 49 days to deliver prototypes and 75 days to complete 70 test vehicles. Specification was four-wheel-drive, crew of three, 2.03m (80in) wheelbase, track no more than 1.1m (47in), empty weight of 590kg (1,300lb), 299kg (660lb) payload and a fold-down windscreen. Karl Probst, a freelance designer, submitted a 'Blitz Buggy' for Bantam, but production contracts went to the bigger manufacturers (now working to a more realistic weight limit of 980kg (2,160lb). Delmar B. 'Barney' Roos and a motley crew of army officers also claimed a design role. Officially the Willys-Overland Military Model MB, it is known everywhere as the Jeep. There is confusion about the origins of the name – it is possibly a phonic contraction of GP (for General Purpose), or possibly came from a Popeye cartoon character, Eugene the Jeep, a name attributed to a rival from the Minneapolis-Moline Power Implement Company (although military slang used 'jeep' to describe anything lazy or worthless). Equally possible as a source for the name is Government Pygmy Willys. The Jeep is an unimprovably simple diagram of its type, but it was consumerized in 1946 into the Jeepster and Station Wagon by designer Brooks Stevens, whose Harley-Davidson ElectraGlide helped to make Milwaukee famous. President Dwight D. Eisenhower said that, along with the C-47 Dakota transport plane, and the bulldozer, the Jeep was the most significant piece of Second World War equipment. 'Jeep' became a registered trademark in 1950. The following year a Jeep was shown in the 'Eight Automobiles' exhibition in New York's Museum of Modern Art. Its purity, longevity and usefulness makes a depressing contrast with its successor, the High Mobility Multipurpose Wheeled Vehicle (HumVee), an RFB of 1981.

1947

Cisitalia

Piero Dusio founded Cisitalia (Consorzio Idustriale Sportivo Italia) in Turin in 1943. He owned the specialist Beltrame bicycle factory which had access to the manufacturing technology and, in particular, the small diameter tubes that made his lightweight cars possible – the famous Cisitalia 202 weighed only 780kg (1,720lb). Dusio hired the best talent to realize his dream of a modern Italian sports car. First engineering studies were by Dante Giacosa, FIAT's visionary engineer. Then Giovanni Savonuzzi was appointed Cisitalia's technical director. It was Savonuzzi who created this beautiful, spare graphic. The Cisitalia was such a technically pure machine that various of the Torinese *carrozzerie* were tempted to enhance it. Alfredo Vignale made some early bodies, but it was when Pininfarina devised a closed coupé body

for the Cisitalia that a landmark in the history of car design was reached. To Savonuzzi's uncompromisingly functional nose, Pininfarina made sensitive, sculptural additions. He suggested a pair of aerodynamic stabilizing fins, but these gave way to integrated wings, making the Pininfarina Cisitalia a wonder of formal composition and a prototype for nearly every Italian sports car of the Fifties (see page 29). Despite its different authors, the Cisitalia appears a superb whole. Only 170 were built between 1947 and 1952, but because one of them was exhibited at the New York's Museum of Modern Art's car design exhibition of 1951, it became one of the most influential automobiles of all time. The Pininfarina Cisitalia was acquired for MoMA'a permanent design and remains there today. Its companions: an E-Type Jaguar and a smart.

1948

Cadillac '61

In 1941 Harley Earl arranged a visit to a secret air-force base so his staff could look at the revolutionary Lockheed P-38 'Lightning', a fighter-bomber with a dramatic twin-boom configuration and gorgeous details including erotic scoops and a blister canopy. He had access because General Motors' Allison Division supplied Lockheed with V-1710-27/29 1150hp V-12 aero engines. They were not allowed to take notes, but they were told to 'mentally recall' every detail. When car production resumed after 1945, Frank Hershey and other GM designers were working on Cadillac's 1949 Model Year 'Futuramic' series and the P-38 was an inspiration. Because of a United Auto Workers' strike, Hershey worked on the car at his home, Winkler Mill, Rochester. When Earl saw the prototype he disparagingly compared it to a turtle. But there was now a new source of semantic inspiration: the 1946 Lockheed Shooting Star jet. The result was the Cadillac '61, a masterpiece of enormous, restrained grandeur. Hershey and his assistant Ned Nickles followed Earl's highlighting principles and obeyed his instruction for the front end to 'look Tiffany'. But aircraft contributed to the continuous, sinuous profile and to those tail fins. Earl's successor as GM design boss, William Mitchell, explained that 'the fins give definition to the rear of the car for the first time. They make the back as interesting as the front.' This car was the beginning of the technicolour adventure of the delirious, uninhibited, guilt-free kitsch that American car design was to become in the Fifties.

1948

Jaguar XK120

This is the car that made Jaguar's reputation. Perhaps the most perfectly complete expression of the English sports car, it is also a fairly complete expression of English genius in all its flawed, opportunistic, eccentric originality. The gorgeous streamlined shape was a sensation when it appeared in the drab, rationed environment of the 1948 London Motor Show. At the time, Elizabeth David was researching her book *Mediterranean Food*, launched two years later into an England that was still eating beige soup and rissoles. The Jaguar was an automotive expression of similar yearnings. But this most English of cars was clearly influenced by the shape of the BMW 328, especially the Mille Miglia specials. Jaguar's presiding genius, Sir William Lyons, said that the XK120 took just two weeks from concept to a full-sized mock-up. The first cars had handmade aluminium panels over an ash frame, but for production the car had a pressed-steel body with aluminium bonnet and doors.

Artistically, it is a satisfying combination of being apparently simple: a clear, unified, flowing form with no fussy effects, but it is also extremely subtle. And, despite the influence of BMW, completely and wholly original. No car body has ever made such voluptuous, but disciplined, use of curves. To build on the sensational consumer response, Jaguar did a well-publicized speed trial. On 30 May 1949, with Ron 'Soapy' Sutton at the wheel, a virtually standard XK120 reached a record speed of 213kp/h (132.6mph) on a Belgian autoroute near Jabbeke, close to Ostend. Lyons observed the achievement of his beautiful car from a chartered Douglas DC-3 circling overhead. In California, taking a break from the movies, Clark Gable road-tested the car for the March 1950 edition of *Road & Track,* announcing himself astonished. Humphrey Bogart was another signatory to the Jaguar cult. The original price of the XK120 was £998.

1948

Land Rover Series 1

The Land Rover Series I is one of the most perfect car designs of all time, but its origins did not lie in a clear brief to a designer of genius, but in a pleasant muddle and in Welsh puddles. Rover's chief designer, Maurice Wilks, had used an American Jeep on his Anglesey farm during the Second World War. Impressed, he decided to better it. The Series I Land Rover used a Willys Jeep chassis and a Rover P3 gearbox. Wilks pioneered recycling with a frugal and ingenious use of military surplus aluminium. Soon Jeep components were being designed out of the Land Rover and it became what German philosophers call a *Ding an sich*, or thing unto itself. By 1950, the stop-gap Land Rover was outselling Rover's conventional cars, the ones legendarily enjoyed by English solicitors. It was the beginning of a design language the company is still using in the twenty-first century. The Series I Land Rover is an extraordinary graphic composition, rather like a child's drawing of a car. It is all straight lines, but utterly distinctive and characteristic. Like the ur-Volkswagen, it is a car that is immediately identifiable in silhouette alone. Gerry McGovern, Land Rover's chief designer in 2008, explained that the Series I achieved this remarkable effect because of its perfect proportions. Overhangs are appropriate to a vehicle of this type and size. Generally, each part is in a nice relationship with the whole. Nothing is oversized, or too diminished. The 1948 car was a masterpiece of vernacular chic: ghosts of it remain in the Land Rover LRX concept shown at the 2008 Detroit Auto Show. McGovern said that this was because the original had 'No Zorro bullshit stuff'.

1949

Porsche 356

Chief Designer Karl Rabe began working on the private project that became the Posrche 356 at Gmund in Carinthia, Germany, in 1946. To this remote spot the Porsche Konstruktionsburo-für-Motoren-Fahrzeug-Luftfahrzeug-und-Wasserhahrzeugbau had removed itself after wartime design consultancy that included the Vergeltungswaffe or V-1 buzz-bomb and Porsche Typ 205, better known as the Maus tank. The Porsche 356 became a reality on 8 June 1948: a two-seater sports car of exceptional lightness and purity of concept. Using standard Volkswagen components, it was designed to achieve ideal performance/weight ratios and to offer minimal resistance to the air. The bonnet of this rear-engined car was not low-slung just for aerodynamic penetration: Porsche theory insisted that the driver should be in emotional contact with the road. The 35hp Number 1 Porsche could reach 135kp/h (84mph). In 1950 Porsche moved to a factory in Zuffenhausen, a Stuttgart suburb, and began series production of the 'German' 356. Bodies, manufactured by Reutter, were to a design by Erwin Komenda, who had drawn the original Volkswagen. The very first production car was known as 'Windhund' (or Wind Hound) on account of its Irish wolfhound coloration. With this car Komenda developed an experimental technical prototype into a mature shape and in so doing created what has become the Porsche signature. Dr Porsche died in January 1951. American importer Max Hoffman told the younger Ferry Porsche, 'That design is absolutely impossible. You will never sell that car in America.' By August of that year, the 1,000th Porsche had been produced. The 356 evolved continuously until the final version was produced in 1965. The absolutely impossible design evolved into the Porsche 911, perhaps the greatest sports car ever made.

1949

Citroën 2CV

Pierre Boulanger's 'umbrella on wheels' had its origins in 1936, an automobile expression of the architectural philosophy of Existenzminimum, or Toute Petite Voiture (TPV), of 1939. Code-named 'Bécassine', or snipe, it was the result of 10,000 opinions sought in a market research exercise unusual for its day. Bauhaus principles of truth to materials and geometrical purity were fundamental to its conception, although the brief was in fact more homespun: the TPV was to carry a *paysan* with 50kg (110lb) of agricultural goods at 50kp/h (31mph). Intended to be light alloy, by the time manufacture was being seriously considered the car was made in steel. The concept was revived after 1945 by Boulanger and engineer André Lefebvre. Launched in 1948 at the Paris Salon (after becoming known as 'Toujours Pas Vue' on account of the production delays), the new Citroën featured aircraft-style tubes under a thin steel carapace. The unique body was designed by Flaminio Bertoni and featured doors and canvas seats that could be removed for a *déjeuner sur l'herbe*. Besides the expressive

Bauhaus logic, there was a practical rationale for its appearance. The semi-unitary body was inexpensive to make as it used mostly flat stampings, also easy to repair. It was held together by a mere 16 bolts. The roof and (originally) the boot lid were canvas. This was both cheap and practical: awkward agricultural objects could easily be accommodated. Prototypes had a single headlamp. A single indicator unit sufficed. There were no expensive window winders, just hinged flaps. Available in any colour so long as it was *gris metallique*, it was met with a mixture of derision and delight. In 1953 a darker grey was introduced with yellow wheels. In the same year the 2CV acquired locks and the cable-pull starter was replaced by an ignition key. In 1955 the AZPL (for '*porte de malle*') model was introduced with the exciting innovation of a metal boot lid. Production ended in 1990. In the same year the TPV was shown at the Salon d'Automobile, Flaminio Bertoni exhibited alongside Giorgio de Chirico at the Salon d'Automne.

1949

Volkswagen

When it arrived in the US in 1953, the wheezing Volkswagen was greeted with comedic distain, but it soon 'transformed national consciousness', in the words of motoring journalist Brock Yates. Its early history goes back to 1925 when Austro-Hungarian engineer Bela Barenyi presented some design proposals for a rear-engined car with a teardrop shape to the Maschinenbauanstalt Wien. At some point, Barenyi's concept seems to have entered German National Socialist consciousness. The Volkswagen we know today was developed for Hitler by Dr Ferdinand Porsche, after a pronouncement from the Führer at the 1934 Berlin Motor Show demanding a car for the Volk that could be bought by customers with a budget of 1000 Reichsmarks, which hitherto gave them access only to a motorbike. Hitler later revealed concern that motorbike users would get wet in rain, imposing inappropriate indignity on the Ubermenschen. The Volkswagen contract was signed on 22 June 1934 with a target price of 990 Reichsmarks. The Porsche design consultancy was given a retainer of 20,000 Reichsmarks

a month to develop prototypes, but this was so exiguous that they were built in the family villa on Stuttgart's Feuerbacher Weg. In 1936 Hitler decided the Volkswagen project should be sponsored by the Kraft durch Freude movement. Early Volkswagens were thus known as the 'Strength through Joy' car, although it was officially Porsche Typ 60. The Volkswagen, later known as the 'Kaefer' (Beetle) had a body designed by Erwin Kommenda on the aerodynamic principles established by Paul Jaray, although the Chrysler Airflow may also have been an influence. The source of Porsche's own-name sports car concept and the inspiration for Doyle Dane Bernbach's superlative ironic advertisements, the Volkswagen's influence was equalled only by the Model T Ford's and the Mini's. In 1955 the State Patent Office in Mannheim accepted that Bela Beranyi had, in fact, designed the Volkswagen. He accepted compensation of a single Deutsche Mark. Beetle production in Germany lasted from 1941 to 1978; it then shifted to Mexico, where the very last car was produced in July 2003.

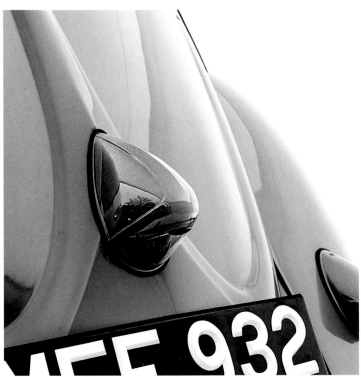

1949

Ford

The '49 Ford was a simple car, but a revolutionary one. *Car and Driver* magazine declared it 'the car that saved Ford'. It is almost impossible to attribute it to a single designer because it was the result of a competition with consultants against in-house designers. Anyway, Ford's Ernest Breech said, 'I have a vision. We start from scratch.' This was not quite true, as everybody in the process was influenced by Raymond Loewy's Studebaker, what Eugene 'Bob' Gregorie called 'that little double-ended Studebaker'. A clay model of the '49 was baked in the kitchen oven of Dick Caleal's home in Mishakawa, Indiana. Meanwhile, a Studebaker was bought, disassembled, weighed and labelled. The single greatest influence may have been consultant George Walker. He made hitherto bulging sides flat and helped to create the simple, elegant, integrated shape. Against this, the spinner nose contrasts nicely. As a result of the '49's success, Walker was appointed Design Director of Ford in 1955. In November 1957 *Time* magazine called him 'The Cellini of Chrome'. In 2001 J Mays showed a retrofuturist '49 at the North American International Auto Show in Detroit. Mays explained 'by really sharpening and paring down the design, a car was created that looked clean, streamlined, modern… it's so much closer to the cars that followed it and so unlike the cars that immediately preceded it.'

1949

SAAB 92

The vehicle manufactured by SAAB before the 92 was the conceptually radical 21 single-seat fighter. Designed by a team led by Frid Warnstrom, the 21 first flew in July 1943. Its general arrangement was gloriously strange: a rear-mounted pusher-propeller was driven by an inverted-V engine. The engine-cockpit unit was a discreet pod between dramatic twin-tail booms. It was evidence of genuine original thinking so, when the aircraft engineers of Svenska Aeroplan AB found themselves redundant in 1945 they decided to make a genuinely original car, the SAAB 92. It was built on aircraft principles with a monocoque structure given emphatic aerodynamic form. With the engine placed ahead of the front axle, the passenger cell and centre of gravity could be low. The 92's engineer was Gunnar Ljungstrom, who worked on the 21's wing structure. Ljungstrom gave the task of body design to Sixten Sason, a Swedish artist who kept an atelier in Paris, but was also well respected as a technical and science fiction illustrator. Early drawings for X9248 (as the project was known internally) were gorgeous gouaches of a terrestrial spaceship occupied by leggy women. Wheel arches were originally faired in, but this was found to have practical disadvantages in the Swedish winter since they unhelpfully allowed snow and mud to accumulate, to the detriment of the steering. For production the design was compromised… but not very much. The 92 that went into production was one of the most advanced small cars ever: an aero-engineer's concept executed by a techno-romantic artist. Sason also designed the body of the Hasselblad camera and the best-known Electrolux vacuum cleaners of the Fifties.

1950

Volkswagen Transporter

The first development of the original Volkswagen car, its van derivative became almost as much of a cult vehicle. The Transporter retained the original Porsche design's logic and purity, but had a commercial character as well. Its origins are due to Ben Pon, an entrepreneur from Amersfoort in the Netherlands. Pon met with British occupation forces on 23 April 1947 to discuss his idea. He had seen a device made by Volkswagen, the Plattenwagen, intended to move goods around the Wolfsburg factory. This was, effectively, a featureless base with an engine attached which was used to shift pallets around the factory floor. It became the ultimate evolution of the Volkswagen idea. Pon wanted a van that weighed 750kg (1,653lb) and could transport the same weight. Two prototypes were made by Volkswagen and tested in a Braunschweig wind-tunnel. These were known as Typ 29, but were aerodynamically unsatisfactory. A more curvaceous proposal by Pon was taken up. Although Pon's sketch was intuitive rather than scientific, the bluff-nosed transporter proved to be more aerodynamic than the Kaefer (Beetle). Notable features were the elegant moulding and the unusually prominent VW logo. The prototype had a wiper for the driver alone. Pon's Transporter achieved an amazing focus on cargo space located precisely between axles, aided by the symmetrical distribution of engine at one end with driver at the other. The Amersfoort entrepeneur's motorized factory pallet evolved into the California surfer-dude's VW Microbus in the Sixties.

1951

Lancia Aurelia B20 GT

Nearly 300 years ago, the yearning for the south led the British to invent tourism and shopping. They called it the Grand Tour. The type of car that later evolved to meet the needs of trans-European travel was called a Gran Turismo in deference to this tradition. Indeed, Anglophile associations with driving across France and Italy became so profound that the leading Milanese *carrozzeria* of the last century called itself Touring, since the English word conjured up notions of style and gentility that, at the time, the Italians felt were beyond their reach. The very first car to be called a GT was the Lancia Aurelia B20, a coupé version of the 1951 Aurelia B10 saloon. The very first cars were manufactured by Carrozzeria Viotti, but Pininfarina soon took over production. Racing successes helped to confirm an image: a two litre B20 came second in the Mille Miglia to a four litre Ferrari. The car was drawn by Mario Boano. Unitary body construction comprised 100 hand-beaten panels, the last time Pininfarina used craft techniques. Although the general arrangement of the fastback coupé never changed,

the B20 went through progressive evolutions up to the Sixth Series; each refined the design and made the car progressively more modern. The First Series B20s were exceptionally austere. The Second Series had a more assertive face with subtly enhanced rear fins. The Third Series appeared in 1953 with wraparound bumpers. The Fourth Series of 1955 is the ultimate B20. There were distinctive push-button door handles and the instrument panel was stylized. Colours were carefully chosen and complementary to cloth trim. Tinted glass was available. The Aurelia B20 GT was the very essence of *bella figura* and defined a lasting automobile type. It was a Lancia B20 which the elder Farina and his son, Sergio, used in 1951 to travel from Turin to Tortona to meet Enzo Ferrari for lunch. Each proud man had been reluctant to play host, but the lunch concluded in an agreement that thereafter Ferarri's image would be managed by the Farina family. The Lancia B20 may thus have been influential in one of the greatest aesthetic adventures of the industrial period.

1952

Bentley R-Type Continental

This was the fastest four-seater car of its day, but also the most elegant and refined. It is the quintessence of English handsomeness, but paradoxically – since it was built for the postwar export drive – none was built for English customers. Its origins were in the postwar Bentley Mark VI, a car designed for economic recovery. It was going to be called a Mark VII, but Jaguar had prior claim to that denomination. The architecture, oddly for something so absolutely English, owes something to contemporary Americana. The source of the profile, with its distinctive fastback, may even be traced to the ineffably proletarian 1949 Chevrolet Fleetline, but there is a general influence from abroad. By the late Forties, car design was going through the equivalent of Dior's New Look in fashion: no longer did passengers sit above the rear axle, as if in a horse-drawn cart. They sat in a lower, sleeker space with a character of its own (in this case that of an English country house). The designer was John Blatchley, who learnt his trade at the traditional Gurney Nutting coachbuilders, where he became chief designer at the age of 23. He joined the aero-engine division of Rolls-Royce, where his aerodynamic improvements to the cowling of the Merlin V-12 gave a distinctive performance advantage to Hurricane and Spitfire fighters during the war. In working on the R-Type Continental, Blatchley used the

Rolls-Royce wind-tunnel; small refinements arising from testing included angling the radiator back an invisible, but aesthetically decisive, three degrees. What was not attributable to the wind-tunnel was attributable to a winning combination of good manners and good taste. The R-Type Continental has an aristocratic bearing, but is at the same time unostentatious and understated. Surfaces are handled with both great confidence and winning tact. Throughout the Fifties, the R-Type Continental was considered one of the most beautiful and desirable cars in the world. When James Bond made his debut in the 1953 book *Casino Royale,* Ian Fleming had him in a fictional 'Bentley Mk IV'. The fantastic Continental was surely the car Fleming had in mind for literature's most famous modern Englishman.

1953

Studebaker Starlight

The Studebaker brothers had made the pioneers' Conestoga wagons. The company had a fine reputation, but always struggled to compete with the American Big Three manufacturers. In the late Thirties management had looked to the emergent design profession for help and found the exotic, flamboyant, self-mythologisizing, perfumed, arrogant, talented Raymond Loewy (who established the first design consultancy in New York in 1927) very willing to help. Loewy opened his own studio with Studebaker's South Bend, Indiana, factory in 1939. It worked in conditions of mythic secrecy with even internal staff subject to punitive security. In 1951, the same year that Loewy published his fabulous, self-serving biography *Never Leave Well Enough Alone*, Studebaker's Harold Vance asked him to produce designs for a two-door four-seater coupé. The result was the 1953 Starlight (which has a B-pillar) and its near-identical twin the Starliner (which is pillarless). The ads said it was 'The new American car with the European look'. Certainly, it had unusual proportions for an American car, and at 142cm (4ft 8in) was dramatically low for its day.

Loewy's design team included Gordon Buehrig (who designed the celebrated Cord) and Albrecht Goertz (who later designed the BMW 507 and Datsun 240Z), although the autograph of the Starlight/ Starliner belonged to Bob Bourke. He explained that 'Loewy never understood sheet metal', but the cars were nonetheless always known as 'the Loewy Coupés'. By a process of recommendation and critique ('Let's just deluxe-y the hell out of these cars'), Loewy exercised his will and the '53 Studebakers were the most complete expression of a designer's concept ever to get into production. Loewy could never distinguish between aesthetic excellence and PR impact, so was delighted when the Starliner appeared on the cover of *Time* magazine for 2 February 1953 with the copyline 'For a sports car era, a long, low whistle-stopper'. In 1955 a near-bankrupt Studebaker had to merge with a near-bankrupt Packard and chrome was lavished on the beautiful Starliner. It was both a proof and a refutation of Loewy's MAYA design principle. The 'Most Advanced Yet Acceptable' was a pleasant delusion.

109 CARS | STEPHEN BAYLEY

1953

Panhard Dyna

Panhard was a pioneer of the French motor industry and, therefore, a pioneer of the automobile itself. René Panhard was an exhibitor at the 1889 Paris Grande Exposition Universelle, the first occasion when the motor industry presented itself as a global force. It was the year the Michelin company was founded. So momentous an event was the Grande Exposition in industrial history that the great tower Gustave Eiffel built for it remains the ultimate expression of the engineering aesthetic. Panhard's cars had a reputation for conceptual eccentricity, sometimes wilfully so. Advertisements declared Panhard '*la doyenne d'avant garde*', although this adventurous design policy eventually led to collapse. The Dyna was Panhard's last successful car, which morphed into the Dyna Z in 1954 and was developed into the mature PL17 in 1959. The original design, conceived under the French government's Pons Plan whereby priority was given to economy cars, was all light alloy, but during its life the panels

progressively became steel (although the engine remained aluminium). The engine and front-wheel-drive power train was in a modular package and the front end lifted as one. The Dyna offered an unrivalled, indeed unique, combination of interior space, ride comfort and economy, this last from an eccentric flat twin engine of improbably small capacity to propel a large car. Efficient aerodynamics, not wholly uncontaminated by the stylist's bravura gestures, helped to achieve this. As did a low weight, 108kg (238lb) for each of six passengers. Curious details included a knob on the steering column to disconnect the battery. And long before such rationality became commonplace, all the Dyna's secondary controls (lights, indicators, acoustic warning) were operated by a single lever. This 850cc car could cruise at 145kp/h (90mph) while carrying four passengers. It was a design masterpiece, but a commercial catastrophe. Panhard was bought by Citroën in 1965 and went out of business two years later.

1953

AC Ace

No car is better evidence of the miscegenated bloodlines and complex lineaments that comprised the mid-century motor industry. Despite its bastard origins, mixed marriages, reckless flirtations and dubious encounters, the AC Ace mutated, by accident and design, into one of the most archetypal sports cars ever. Rather as Jean Lorrain once said, a bad reputation never did anyone any harm. The original AC company was an antique survival of pioneer British vehicle manufacturing. Based in sleepy Thames Ditton, Surrey, it survived thanks to a contract to produce dreadful three-wheeler invalid carriages for the British government. At least, that was true until 1963 when a Texan chicken farmer and racing driver called Carroll Shelby (who had won the 1959 Le Mans 24-hour race driving an Aston Martin DB3S) had the happy idea of inserting a powerful American Ford '289' V-8 into the hitherto unassuming AC Ace. He named it the Cobra. At the time of its introduction, AC was still using a six-cylinder engine

whose history went back to 1919. The Ford engine had a transformational effect on the Ace's performance, but there were other sorts of alchemy involved as well. The Ace's distinguished aspect (so apparently an English classic) is in fact a blatant copy of Carrozzeria Touring's 1949 body design for Ferrari's Barchetta 166 (so-called because it was like a 'little boat'). Other elements in the brew included a tubular chassis by a Cambridge-based Portuguese artisan-designer called John Tojeiro. But, by some mysterious processes not fully understood, the Cobra became much more than the sum of its parts. Shelby employed some of the graphic language of American hot-rodding to turn a well-mannered English sports car into a swollen phallus of visual aggression. Ride height was lowered and wheel arches enhanced snugly to accommodate dramatic dragster wheels and tyres. Scoops were enlarged, ducts added, chrome details judiciously employed. The Cobra influenced nothing, but was an exquisite example of itself.

1953

Chevrolet Corvette

The 'vette was America's first sports car, a Detroit response to the waves of sporty, small British two-seaters which had started the California sports car cult in the years after 1945. It was shown to the public on 16 January 1953 in the Motorama, one of Harley Earl's famous roadshows, held in the Ballroom of New York's Waldorf Astoria Hotel. On sale six months later, it was the first production car anywhere to have plastic body panels (although the chassis was resolutely old-regime steel). Chevrolet's parent, General Motors, had been the first manufacturer to understand the practicalities and psychology of colour when it began to exploit the new DuPont lacquers in the late Twenties. The first batch of Corvettes was all Polo white with Sportsman red vinyl interiors (the names are revealing of social ambitions). Styling was a shameless display of sexual suggestiveness: the soft red cockpit within a white body may have been unconscious, but was nonetheless dramatically effective. Details were stolen from racing cars and curves were lascivious, but the appearance flattered only to disappoint; with its lazy two-speed Powerglide transmission and unfit 'stovebolt' 3.5-litre six cylinders, known melodramatically as Blue Flame Six, this automobile equivalent of the psychodrama of sex was embarrassingly slow. Not even Harley Earl's evocative jet nozzles could help, and despite a modest $3,250 price, the Corvette was a market failure until in 1955 Chevrolet's small block V8 was fitted and performance was radically enhanced. The Corvette was completely reskinned for 1956, with better colours, more body sculpting, more chrome, but still faithful to Earl's gloriously vulgar original. In 1960 the car was canonized by the *Route 66* television show. It was America at its best, a product of the innocent and optimistic mid-Fifties when consumer dreams of the past came true, but a sense of a new future was there for all who cared. 'Who barreled down the highways of the past journeying to each other's hot-rod Golgotha', wrote Allen Ginsberg in *Howl* in 1955–6. The Beats may not have cared for the Corvette, but – queasily – they shared the same culture.

1954

Mercedes-Benz 300SL

No single car better demonstrates the consummate, almost arrogant, German mastery of automobile art and technology than the Mercedes-Benz 300SL. The SL stands for 'Sport Leicht' or light sports car, but that's only a small part of the story. Up to the Second World War, Mercedes-Benz had a superb reputation for making limousines, trucks and racing cars. After the war, the company continued Hitler's Silber Pfeilen (Silver Arrows) racing policy, but this time in pursuit of commercial markets, not military conquests. In 1952 Mercedes-Benz won the famous Le Mans 24-hour race and the US importer Max Hoffmann told the Stuttgart factory he could sell a thousand domesticated racing cars in America, if they could build them. This task fell to designer Friedrich Geiger with engineers Karl Wilfert and Walter Hacker. Two years after the Le Mans victory, a house-trained version

of the racing car came to market. Signature features included 'gull wing' doors hinged at the roof, made necessary by the longitudinal pontoons, which provided a rigid structure but made conventional doors unfeasible. Details included trapezoidal intakes, a company motif and curious eyebrows over wheel arches. The engine was canted at a 45-degree angle which allowed a dramatically low bonnetline. Not entirely innocent of the temptations of beautiful empty gestures, Bracq included an additional power bulge on the bonnet to create a pleasing symmetry. The whole is an exquisite sculpture of total originality: although the racing car was the starting point, the destination was quite new. Crisp details give a confident, graphic clarity. Long before 'branding' became an issue, the 300SL made emphatic use of Mercedes-Benz' three-pointed star.

1954

Ford Thunderbird

The Ford Thunderbird is a perfect representative of the age of innocent consumer excess that Tom Wolfe called 'America's Bourbon Louis romp'. The year after its introduction, the United States made more cars than ever before or since. It was conceived as a competitor for Chevrolet's Corvette, but had the advantage of a powerful V-8 engine as opposed to Chevrolet's crude and wheezy six. Original names included Hep-Cat, El Tigre and Detroiter, but when one of the design team, Alan Giberson, remembered seeing a bird struck by lightning with notable explosive effect, he had an inspiration which, vouchsafed in a Dearborn meeting room, became immortal. He was rewarded with a $95 Saks suit. The Thunderbird is total, vulgarian confectionery. It has dummy bonnet scoops. Some versions had 'opera' windows. All versions were seductive: chief designer Franklin Hershey, ex Cadillac '48, a member of the extended Ford family, defined the idea of a 'personal' car, one that was mass-produced but with a bespoke feel. Marilyn Monroe owned a pink one, in a Detroit–Hollywood take on sympathetic magic. Thunderbird demonstrated Ford's understanding of consumer psychology and how meaning can be differentiated by details: a 'Continental' option was chosen by Norma Jean. This included an irrational, but gorgeous, external spare wheel with a hard cover. Other versions had restricted use of chrome. Hershey said that he wanted a banker to feel dignified in a Thunderbird. When Allen Ginsberg wrote his epic poem *Howl* in 1955–6, he caught the mood that made the Thunderbird possible: 'Robot apartments Invisible suburbs! Skeleton treasuries! Blind capitals! Demonic industries! Spectral nations! Invincible madhouses! Granite cocks!' When the Beachboys sang, 'We'll have fun, fun, fun 'till daddy takes the T-bird away', this was the car they were thinking of.

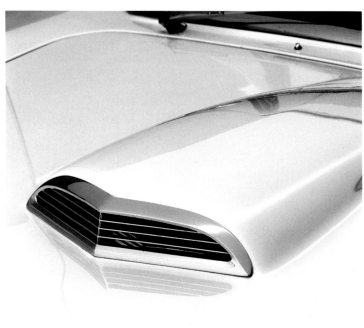

1954

Alfa Romeo Giulietta Sprint

This was the response by Carrozzeria Bertone to rival Pininfarina's Lancia B20, the original Gran Turismo of four years before. The Giulietta was conceived as a moderately priced, but supremely elegant, addition to Alfa Romeo's range. More mass-market than the aristocratic Lancia, in a sense the little Giulietta is the predecessor of all the best small coupés from the second half of the twentieth century: a small two-plus-two, almost effeminately elegant with discreet and modest details within a finely proportioned whole. Launched in the year that Federico Fellini premiered his dark road movie, *La Strada*, the exquisitely pretty Giulietta Sprint anticipated the more optimistic *dolce vita* just around the corner. As a package, it offered the newly emerging Italian middle-class consumer access to a world of sophistication hitherto restricted to a privileged few. As a work of art, it represents Bertone's offer to the consumer of the extravagant aesthetic language he had developed in the BAT (Berlina

Aerodinamica Technica) show cars he used to trail his coat in the same year. First versions of the Giulietta Sprint were partially aluminium, and Perspex filled the daylight openings. Popular success meant that this specification was soon value-engineered to steel and glass. There were some special editions, noteworthy most of all for breakthrough nomenclature: the estate car version by Carrozzeria Boneschi was called La Weekendina. Another estate car version was made in a very short series of 91 by Carrozzeria Boneschi. This remarkable car was called the Giulietta Promiscua, which may or may not have been an amusing Shakespearean reference. Production ran to 1962 when it was replaced by the Giulia, drawn by Bertone's most successful employee, Giorgetto Giugiaro. It is irresistible to suggest that growing up in the studio that created this perfect little car gave Giugiaro the cultural credentials that helped him to become, by the mid-Seventies, the greatest Italian car designer of them all.

1955

Lancia Aurelia B24

Lancia's reputation has become mired and confused by years of lacklustre product dictated by opportunistic corporate managers, not inspired by engineers or talented designers. At the same time, a retreat from US and British markets caused by suboptimal consumer response to ruinous problems with rust and reliability has turned it into a ghost brand. But there was a time when 'Lancia' was a synonym for supreme elegance and high performance contained in packages defined by voluptuous, yet dignified, metal. Lancia also made racing cars at least the equal in glory and speed of those by Ferrari and Alfa Romeo. The Aurelia Spider was launched when Lancia was at the peak of its performance. It was specifically designed for the American market, although first shown at Brussels in 1955 (with atrocious fake-wire wheels). Because of American demands, the B24 was rather larger than previous Lancia sports cars. Also with a nod to the US market, Pininfarina clearly construed it as a less expensive Ferrari and provided bodywork obviously inspired by the Ferrari 375 'America'. The bravura (and very American) wraparound windshield of the show car was abandoned for 1956 and flapping Perspex side-screens replaced by wind-up glass. Door apertures became more generous, but a fundamental elegance remained: it is an aristocrat, but with a lascivious air. It is the car Grace Kelly and Cary Grant used in their Riviera romp, Alfred Hitchcock's *To Catch a Thief* (1955), a film with its own lascivious air: on a picnic Kelly asks Grant if he wants breast or leg. When she fails to seduce him, the film shows her fondling an umbrella. This occult eroticism was surely a projection of the Lancia's character.

1955

MGA

The distinctive MG octagonal badge (rumoured to have been inspired by a plan of Abingdon Prison's Panopticon) was, in fact, an Art Deco confection drawn in 1923 by company accountant Edmund Lee. The spirit of MG is rooted in the mid-Twenties when the Paris Exposition des Arts Décoratifs gave its name to cheerful, content-free *modernisme*. The letters stand for Morris Garages and the badge was first seen on an MG 14/40 Mark IV in 1928, an assemblage of humdrum Morris components turned by alchemy and ingenuity into a passable sports car. Up to the mid-Fifties, MG produced uncomplicated two-seaters with an uncompromisingly *retardataire* style: the TC, TD and TF were the Old English Perpendicular of sports cars. There were no voluptuous curves, no stylist's conceits, but their charm, simplicity and quintessentially English pragmatism made them the basis of California's sports car cult, as well as those of Long Island's North Shore and Connecticut's Fairfield County where imports were favoured by US sophisticates. Without MG, there would never have been Corvettes or Thunderbirds. The MGA represented a break with tradition as disconcerting as if the aircraft industry had gone from a string 'n' canvas Sopwith Camel to a streamlined Hawker Hunter without passing through any intervening stages. It arose from Syd Enever's attempts to do an all-enveloping race-car body for the old sit-up-and-beg TD. It did not work out, so he started again. The MGA was shockingly radical for MG: its first car with a full-width body. Drawing with tact and restraint, the anonymous draughtsman was sure that he could achieve his effects through understatement and well-judged radii rather than showy flourishes. With intuitive aerodynamics, low aspect and modest details, it was outstandingly modern for its day (even if the components remained antique). The US advertisements said 'Designed to steal your heart…There's promise of action in every line.' The MGA was the last admired product of the famous Oxfordshire company.

1955

FIAT 600

Like the original Zero-A (which became the inimitable Topolino), the 600 was designed by the great FIAT engineer Dante Giacosa. And like the Vespa motor scooter, it was one of the machines that defined Italy's industrial revolution. Once, an Italian would make only one or two journeys in his life, either to emigrate or to do military service. The Seicento gave ordinary Italian people freedom and independence: it was a car for Italians who were all first-time buyers. The 600 was designed to replace the antique Cinquecento Belvedere, or estate car. Giacosa built a life-size plaster model to determine the most efficient space utilization. A part of the cost-cutting brief was to minimize use of sheet metal, so bonnet and boot were atrophied, no metetricious details allowed. 'I progressively eliminated all the edges,' Giacosa wrote. He chipped away at the model, producing an elemental, but visionary, design: highly original, but somehow utterly familiar. Even the engine was simplified. Giacosa said, 'As soon as I saw even the very slightest chance of simplification, the design was changed.' The 600 was copied in the Soviet Union as the Zaporozhets ZAZ965.

1955

Citroën DS

Perhaps the single greatest automobile design of all time, the DS is an *objet superlatif*, the exaltation of glass. In a way, it was a product of what Curnonsky called '*la sainte alliance*' between gastronomy and tourism. When André Citroën's prodigal creativity drove Citroën into bankruptcy in 1934, the company was bought by the Michelin Tyre Company. Monsieur Bibendum was the device that encouraged motorists to travel to eat. We call the DS a Citroën, but it might as well be a Bibendum. An advanced flat six engine was planned for this car, but budget constraints meant it actually used the same one as the 1934 Traction Avant. But budget was the only constraint: in every other respect, the DS was the most extreme, advanced and accomplished car ever made. And the body was drawn by the same man, Flaminio Bertoni. In 1938 Pierre Boulanger had started a notebook dedicated to the Voiture de Grande Diffusion. He said to his team, 'Study all the possibilities, including the impossible.' Boulanger was killed in 1950

while testing the car, but he had already refined the brief: 'The world's most beautiful, most comfortable and most advanced car, a masterpiece to show the world… that Citroën and France could develop the ultimate vehicle.' Bertoni achieved the greatest ever work of automobile art. 'Déesse' meant Goddess. First shown without wheels and tyres so as not to compromise the consumers' perception of its pure sculptural form, it was the car that inspired Roland Barthes. 'Smoothness,' Barthes knew, 'is always an attribute of perfection.' High-pressure hydraulics. Self-levelling. Power brakes operated by a button. Automatic clutch. Single-spoke steering wheel. Voluptuously upholstered, astonishing ride. Genuine luxe. Plastic roof with distinctive high level indicators, rumoured to have been a late addition when the plastic roof panels distorted to leave an ugly gap. Barthes rhapsodized over the joins. Gavin Lyall wrote tellingly of it in *The Most Dangerous Game* (1964). But Barthes must have the last word: the DS was the very essence of petit-bourgeois advancement.

1955

BMW 507

BMW's department of Künstlerische Gestaltung, one of the first of its kind, a forerunner of contemporary styling departments, was established in Munich in 1938. Its only significant products before the Second World War were Meyerhuber's streamlined special-bodied 328s which raced in the Mille Miglia. These cars may have inspired the postwar Jaguar XK120, but it was only in the mid-Fifties that BMW was, once again, able to reestablish an authentic artistic direction of its own. In the Fifties the chief artistic influence on BMW was not so much its own German inheritance from the Bauhaus as the twin influences of the American market and Italian style. Indeed, Pininfarina had even made proposals for BMW's first postwar saloon car, the 501. These were more or less ignored and the 501 that went into production was as bloated as a Jodelstil cabinet and became known as the Baroque Angel. One of the first cars to point the way to BMW's future was the gorgeous, egregious 507, almost a Bavarian Corvette. It was designed by Dr Albrecht Graf von Goertz, a colourful individual whose gene

pool was deeply German and aristocratic, but infiltrated by currents from America. The 507 was, after all conceived at the same moment that artists in Britain were, through the medium of Pop, celebrating the flashy, seductive vulgarity of American culture. Von Goertz had worked in the United States with Raymond Loewy on the Studebaker Starliner and later contributed to the Porsche 911; after 1973, when he became a consultant to Datsun (now Nissan), he was responsible for the 240Z of 1966, the first mass-produced Japanese car to acquire cachet in America and Europe. But BMW's first postwar sports car was von Goertz' masterpiece. The 507 uses explicitly American details (the louvres, the chrome, the spinners) and emphatic American form (at the time it was produced, most of BMW's production was tiny *Kleinwagen*). The 507 is significant as a symbol of Germany moving away from austerity towards the enlarged possibilities of the Wirtschaftswunder. It is also significant as a European designer's projection of American fantasies.

1956

Volvo Amazon 120

'Vackrare vardagsvara!' was the slogan of the Swedish design movement. Loosely translated, it is a demand for 'more beautiful everyday things'. That was in 1919. The motor industry being more conservative, it took a while for the message to enter the system. Another way of putting it is to say that up to the launch of the 120, Volvo cars had been plug ugly. Indeed, so entrenched was the culture of anti-glamour that when designer Jan Wilsgaard presented early proposals for the 120 to the company's founders Gustaf Larson and Assar Gabrielsson, the latter commented, 'There is too much of the pin-up about it. It would be better if it was ugly rather than too beautiful.' Critics in 1956 saw both Italian and American influence (Wilsgaard was, coincidentally, born in the United States and the very first Volvos had been innocent copies of tough Chevrolets).

The 120 was the first beautiful Volvo. It has a coupé-like glasshouse, an elegant profile, a distinctive face (with pescatorial nostrils) and just enough chrome to be interesting. It was the first Volvo available in two-tone paint. But, in proper accord with the Swedish design movement, special attention was paid to the interior. The instrumentation was sensibly grouped in front of the driver and there were the first, tentative safety features: padding on the doors and standard seat-belt anchors. Later versions had the very first seat to be designed on ergonomic principles: variable resistance foam was covered with perforated vinyl. The lumbar support (adjustable, at first, only with a screwdriver) was made an explicit visual feature. Upholstery was available in all-black, a radical feature at the time. The 120 was known as the Amazon (originally spelt with an 's'). Publicity material showed models dressed up as Scythian women in tunics and sandals, carrying swords and still, apparently, carrying two breasts even though veracity would have required one since true Amazons were fighting women who cut off a breast the better to draw a bow. Be that as it may, the Amazon established Volvo's enduring brand values.

1956

FIAT Multipla

The FIAT Multipla predicted the international phenomenon of the 'people mover', although it had its own Italian predecessors. The first is an extraordinary 1913 Castagna-bodied Alfa Romeo built for Count Ricotti (now in the company museum in Arese); the second, Count Mario Revelli de Beaumont's design studies for a taxi of 1934. Each was well known in Italian design circles. Forward control made the Multipla an exceptional achievement in packaging: a six-seater within an overall length of 3.5m (11½ft), the Multipla's astonishing single-volume unitary body used the components of the successful 600. There were four-, and five-seat and taxi variants available, all offering ingenious variations of the seating arrangements: with all but the front two seats removed, the tiny Multipla had a loading area of more than 1.7sq/m (18sq/ft). Sold to the public in a charming palette of *gelato* colours, the Multipla made its international debut in 1960 when FIAT supplied the cars to athletes and officials at the Rome Olympics.

1957

Chevrolet Bel Air

Until the mid-Fifties, US cars were painted in drab colours, then chartreuse, aqua, pink, coral and baby blue became available. The Bel Air was available in most of these and in most conceivable two-tone variations, not all of them sanctioned by good taste. This car, named after an expensive Los Angeles suburb, was a dream car made real. Technologically, it was a vehicle that carried new industry standards, including automatic transmission and power-assisted steering and brakes. Artistically, it represented the ultimate mass-market offer of Harley Earl's concept of styling.

'Will we stroll dreaming of the lost America of love past blue automobiles in driveways, home to our silent cottage?' Thus Allen Ginsberg in 'A Supermarket in California', in 1955.

Harley Earl's design team comprised Clare MacKichan, Chuck Stebbins, Bob Verkyzer and Carl Renner. The grille was inspired by Ferrari and one commentator spoke of the da Vinci sculpted door handles. All General Motors designers worked to Earl's brief of going all the way, then backing off some. But the Bel Air team did not back off very much at all.

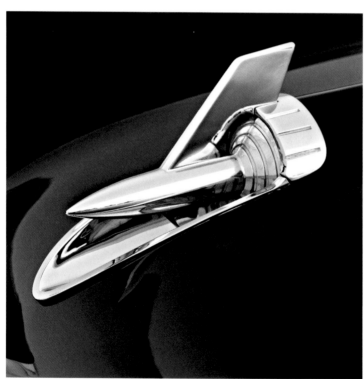

1957

Ford Fairlane 500 Skyliner

Ford had experimented with transparent roofs as early as 1954: access to sunshine was a new variation on the consumer's experience of the automobile. Dealers found they could draw more (male) customers into showrooms with convertibles. Ernest Dichter, President of the Institute for Motivational Research, was commissioned to do some research and discovered that men thought of a convertible as a mistress. It was a lust-filled daydream that lured them into the showroom. Retractable hardtops were the next development. Experiments began at Ford's premium Lincoln Division, but went to market on the mid-range Fairlane. The retractable roof mechanism was ingenious, but complex: a Mahler Fifth of electrical motors, servos, levers and hinges. It added a $350 supplement to the price at a time when the safety-conscious customer could specify seatbelts for $9. Styling features included a clean, full-width chrome grille, twin headlights and graphic side scallop to emphasize two-tone paintwork. Fairlane was the name of Henry Ford's family home in County Cork, Ireland.

1957

Lotus Elite

The car properly known as a Lotus Type 14 is a rare example of an accountant having a beneficial influence in the automobile industry. Peter Kirwan-Taylor was an old-school City man who helped to arrange financing for Colin Chapman's Lotus Car Company. (Chapman was ever a perfect example of someone whose reach far exceeded his grasp.) Kirwan-Taylor drew the first version of the car that is routinely described as one of the most beautiful ever made. It was also one of the most technologically advanced: Chapman was always influenced by aerospace practice and had a fanatical interest in lightness, sometimes at the cost of integrity. Kirwan-Taylor's Elite was the first car ever to have a fully stressed fibreglass monocoque structure. (The 1953 Chevrolet Corvette had used fibreglass panels, but they were mounted on a separate steel frame.) As a result, the Elite weighed little more than 455kg (1,000lb) – but the cars suffered problems with flexing and cracking. The resin used to fix the fibreglass also had an unfortunate propensity to catch fire. Some of these problems were fixed when Kirwan-Taylor's design proposals were revised by Frank Costin, chief aerodynamicist of the de Havilland Aircraft Company. To continue the aeronautical association, later versions of the Elite were manufactured by the Bristol Aeroplane Company.

But it was Kirwan-Taylor whose creativity extended to getting this utopian project into production. The fibreglass monocoque technology forced an aesthetic simplicity: there were no sharp angles or intrusive perforations. But an original designer's eye forced unusual fineness on the car. The Elite is a composition that is balanced and elegant. Chapman's motto was 'simplify and add lightness'. Kirwan-Taylor added unusual beauty as well. The Elite is a design from which nothing might beneficially be taken nor to which anything (apart from a rigid backbone) might beneficially be added. Thanks to time spent in aeronautical labs, the car had an astonishingly low drag-coefficient of .29. In the same spirit of improvisational genius that made the Spitfire the finest fighter aircraft, the Coventry-Climax engine used in the Elite was derived from the unit used in a firefighter's pump.

1957

FIAT 500

This car was defined by the Italian townscape: perhaps the smallest viable four-seater ever, it could cope with narrow streets. It was also designed for Italian life: a product conceived without cynicism, but with a simple passion. This 'nuova' Cinquecento was the successor to Dante Giacosa's original Zero-A or Topolino of 1936. The brief during the period of *ricostruzione*, when Italy had its industrial revolution, was that 'every worker should have a car'. Accordingly, simplicity and economy were decisive. Giacosa was also responsible for the 500. He had a fundamentalist disapproval of excess and spoke of the inspiration he received from the quest for simplicity. He understood the techniques of body construction and designed panels that were cheap to make, but that did not mean they were dull. On the contrary, the quest for economy of means stimulated genius. The 500 has nearly flat glass, but clever pinching and contouring of the body panels makes the whole appear as a generous – if tiny – sculpture, not as a frugal box. Giacosa grew to dislike computers, saying that they were 'only capable of rapidly verifying results, not of anticipating them'. Even more so than its predecessor, the 600, the Cinquecento revolutionized Italian social life. It won a Compasso d'Oro in 1959 and remained in production until 1975. In 2007 FIAT revived the Cinquecento with a design by Roberto Gioleti, which pays frank homage to Giacosa's original.

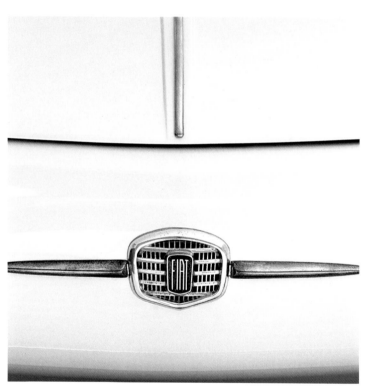

1958

Nash Metropolitan

The Nash Metropolitan (from Birmingham) first greeted the public as the experimental Nash-Kelvinator NX1 at New York's Waldorf-Astoria Hotel on 5 January 1950. It was early evidence of Jetsons-era modernity that defined that largely optimistic decade. Unusual for an American car of its day, the NX1 attempted technological economy within an artistically unusual package. At a moment when the major manufacturers were essaying the prospects of demented excess, the NX1 was designed to meet unusual criteria, including dignity and economy. The prototype was shown in a deep shade of maroon, itself an unusual choice. The design of the actual body was even more unusual. It had integrated front bumpers and the entire front-body assembly opened as a single unit. There was no exterior boot lid and access to the luggage space was via the interior. These economies meant an astonishingly low weight of 612kg (1,350lb). The style was wholly original with neither predecessor nor, it must be admitted, followers.

Originally powered by a FIAT engine, the NX1 was trailed around the continental United States in a series of customer events called 'surviews', as cute as the car itself. In a survey 90 per cent of correspondents said they 'approved' of its design, although subsequent sales figures did not confirm this early excitement. In March 1954 the NX1 crossed the Atlantic to become the Austin Metropolitan, after designer Bill Fajole had been given a Lucas headlamp bezel and asked to adapt the NX1 architecture to this British component (which he described as 'lousy'). While conceived as an offer of European discipline in the US market, in Britain the little Nash (as it became known) was wistfully interpreted as a miniature of Americana: a moderne hardtop with two-tone vinyl upholstery and ice-cream palette for exterior paint. Its contemporary was the Hillman Californian, a Minx chopped and changed and touched by Raymond Loewy's garish genius.

1959

Jaguar Mark II

The Mark II was the evolution of Jaguar's compact car, the 2.4 litre Mark I that was launched in September 1955, just a few months after a Jaguar D-Type won the 24-hour Le Mans race. Like the D-Type racing car, the compact saloon had unitary or aircraft-style 'monocoque' construction. This technology made cars light and strong and had a subtle influence on aesthetics. When cars had separate chassis, there was a tendency to construe the body as separate architecture, but this car was conceived as a whole. William Lyons called it the 'rotund look'. A comparison with its exact contemporary, the Citroën DS, is instructive. The Jaguar's formal language depends on prominent, generously curved front wings that take a line rearwards into an elegantly sloping torpedo tail. For the 1960 Model Year,

Jaguar introduced this car: the Mark II compact had a bigger 3.8 litre engine, but the aesthetics had been brightened and tightened too. Window area had grown, pillars were thinner, ovoid grille more egregious, chrome highlights tipping the car towards the raffish personality it later defined among its customers.

Compact Jaguars were extremely successful in motor racing and rallying, contributing generously to the company's fast, accumulating fund of image capital. The Mark II defined the concept of the English sports saloon. Best seen in British racing green with red leather upholstery and chrome wire wheels, it lasted until 1969, by which time it seemed an elegiac memento of a lost England.

1959

Volvo P1800

The P1800 was Volvo's first sports car, designed as an image-builder for the company as a whole. The Ghia and Frua *carrozzerie* made early submissions for a two-seat coupé based on Amazon mechanicals, but management chose a car designed in-house by Pelle Petterson (who later devoted himself to naval architecture and the Americas Cup). Photos of the 1959 prototype showed a car very close to the one that went into production two years later. The P1800 has dramatic proportions with an enormous bonnet (way too commodious for the humble four-cylinder engine it houses, but it is there to suggest ample power) and a small, low glasshouse placed well back. Surfaces are complex with wonderfully curious changes of radius and direction: the beltline turns from a roll to a razor edge as it moves rearwards. Critics thought the chrome emphasis on

the flanks an error of taste, although it proved distinctive. The front fenders and lights have a striking prognathous look; the grille is expressive. Inside, it is an exercise in controlled Americana: prominent instrument bezels, emphatic use of pleats and plastic. An opening rear window had always been an intention, but this was realized only when the Coggiola company of Turin showed a P1800 'ES' prototype in 1968, a coupé with a load deck – the first car in this format. The image-building role of the Volvo P1800 was dramatically enhanced through product placement. Roger Moore starred in the television series based on Leslie Charteris' louche detective, *The Saint*. He had wanted a Jaguar for the part, but Jaguar could not deliver. Volvo, at the time assembled by Jensen in West Bromwich, obliged. Moore's white P1800 gave the dour Volvo company an improbable reputation for glamour.

1959

Chevrolet Corvair

Chevrolet engineers began experimenting with a rear-engined design code-named Cadet just after 1945, but a buoyant market for conventional cars was no incentive to experiment. But by the later Fifties, the success of the Volkswagen Beetle had forced a revision. The air-cooled, rear-engined Corvair may have been influenced by Porsche's Volkswagen in terms of general arrangement. The engine itself may have been influenced by the classic Lycoming aircraft engine. It was known, at least in some quarters, as the 'Waterless Wonder from Willow Run'. But, while radical, the Corvair had neither Porsche's dynamic integrity nor aerospace's quintessential lightness. Indeed, the value-engineered and underspecified swing-axle rear suspension together with an overweight engine contributed to the series of accidents that made the Corvair the subject of Ralph Nader's consumerist polemic, *Unsafe at Any Speed* (1965). But, safety apart, it was positively outstanding. The 900 Monza (originally a special edition created by designer Bill Mitchell for his daughter) led the market as a sporty compact with pleated bucket seats, a concept that influenced the more conservative Mustang. A gear shifter on the floor, psychologist Joyce Brothers explained, was an expression of male sexuality. Meanwhile, the crisp, European lines of Ned Nickles with the big glasshouse and emphatic beltline were a profound influence on Sixties BMWs. Lights were, influentially, treated as jewellery. In May 1965 Dr Seymour Charles, founder of Physicians for Automotive Safety, spoke at Detroit's Cobo Hall and demanded a total recall of all Corvairs. More poetically, a woman with experience of the car's dynamic shortcomings described a drive in a Corvair as a 'sashay through the boonies, back-end first'. It was a revolutionary design in every sense.

1959

Austin A40

The civilization that brought Britain the Kenwood Chef and the first supermarkets also produced the Austin A40. It was Leonard Lord of the old British Motor Corporation who inspired two completely different products, each launched in 1959. The first was the radical Morris Mini Minor (later the 'Mini'), the second was the more technologically conservative Austin A40. It was based on the quaint Austin A35 (whose bulbous body was designed by a Birmingham-based Italian called Riccardo Burzi, inspired by a Lancia original. But Lord hired Pininfarina to create an exceptionally modern shape for the A40. With its fine proportions, razor-edged styling and unique hatchback (in the Countryman version), it suddenly graduated from being merely utilitarian to desirable. The A40 hinted at a notion that did not exist in 1959: lifestyle. Pininfarina had begun to make English contacts in 1957 when he had been voted a Royal Designer for Industry. The year before, he had begun his ambitious collaboration with Peugeot, the first manufacturer to bring his work to the mass market. It is wonderfully eloquent of the almost surreal complexities of car design that in the same year the A40 was shown at Earl's Court, Pininfarina also showed its greatest ever project: the Ferrari 250GT.

1959

Mini

The Mini is one of a handful of the great, undisputed car designs of all time. It is an example of the synoptic genius of Alec Issigonis, a martinet, intolerant of authority and hierarchy. Issigionis' design was stimulated by the 1956 fuel crisis caused by the Suez invasion, but he was determined that it should not be a crude 'bubble' car. The Mini had to conform to the stern brief he set himself. A man preoccupied with the intelligent use of space, Issigonis had a concept of a car only 3m (10ft) long, but with 80 per cent of its length devoted to passengers. To achieve this, he turned the engine sideways. The 24cm (10in) wheels limited intrusion into the passenger cell and gave the car a unique stance. The gearbox was expensively, but ingeniously, placed within the engine's crankcase. He expressed economy by exposed welding flanges on the bodywork. There were sliding windows and plastic string door pulls. But among these explicit austerities, the minuscule Mini had astonishing internal storage for people and things. However, the uncompromising Issigonis believed it was safer for the driver to be uncomfortable so he deliberately chose an awkward driving position. The transverse engine may owe its origins to Gerald Palmer, responsible for the failed (but remarkable) 1947 Jowett Javelin, before the Mini the most radical British car of all time. The Mini's distinctive body was a scaled-down version of the XC9001, an abortive project of 1956. Issigonis eschewed styling but achieved unconscious chic.

Because it was so radical, the Mini was impossible for a snobbish British consumer to categorize and thus, astonishingly, became the first small car to be perceived as classless. No one said it at the time, but in the Mini great design proved to be universally alluring.

1959

Cadillac Eldorado Biarritz

This is Harley Earl, chief wizard in the den of kitsch that was mid-century Detroit, at his delirious best: the ultimate in auto baroque. From the restrained grandiosity of the '48 Cadillac, Harley Earl drove the company through an ever tightening helix of inventiveness. Rapidly evolving Cadillac form was the pink and chrome illustration of planned obsolescence (although they preferred to call it the 'dynamic economy'). By the mid-Fifties, Cadillac bumpers had outrageous projecting cones, known as 'Dagmars' after the one-name star of the late-night television series *Broadway Open House*; Dagmar was known for her provocative bosom. Cadillac advertisements spoke of 'inherent dignity and grace and beauty'. That cliff of chrome was meant to transmit notions of solidity and endurance. The interior offered 'lasting luxury and beauty'. The '59 Cadillac was chosen by

Life magazine as the cover shot for an issue devoted to the century of the automobile. In 1959 such a choice made sense. The '59 Cadillacs pioneered cruise control, almost a metaphor of the garish, somnolent arrogance which defines the car and, perhaps, its customers. So emphatically American, the nomenclature betrayed incongruous yearnings for an exotic Europe so conceptually distant from the Mid-West. Biarritz was the convertible; Seville, the hardtop. This is the car which, when painted in Du Pont's mountain laurel pink, inspired Sammy Master's rockabilly hit as well as Bruce Springsteen's suggestive lyrics: 'Riding in the back/Oozing down the street/Waving to the girls/Feeling out of sight/Spending all my money on a Saturday night'. A pink cadillac embodies the American concept of luxury and style at mid-century: untested, unexamined, gross, inimitable, unforgettable and unique.

1961

Lincoln Continental

The '61 Lincoln, launched the year Ernest Hemingway shot himself, the same year that 'Runaround Sue' was a hit, was the first US car to escape the Golden Age of Gawp, the artistic language of 'Detroit Machiavellismus'. The Lincoln is a complete original, but shares significant morphological details with the pillbox hat of one of its most famous passengers, Jackie Kennedy. (The hat was a design by Oleg Cassini, whose brother coined the expression 'Jet Set'.) Considered as a formal composition, the Lincoln disguises its vast bulk with exquisite proportions and bravely undecorated surfaces. Like a Donald Judd sculpture, metal is allowed to express itself in bold horizontals. The brightwork on the fenderline emphasizes plastic confidence rather than exaggerated glitz. The massive grille is chrome, but well-mannered. This is the car that pioneered curved sideglass, giving it dramatic tumblehome. Its designers Eugene Bordinat, Don De La Rossa, Elwood P. Engle, Gayle L. Halderman, John Najjar, Robert M. Thomson and George Walker won the US Industrial Design Institute Award for Overall Excellence. The dark blue example John Kennedy used was painted funereal black after the events on Dallas' Deeley Plaza.

1961

Jaguar E-Type

The Jaguar E-Type was the most exciting and beautiful car ever designed for mass-production. It was launched at the Parc des Eaux Vives, a Geneva lakeside hotel. An evolution of the D-Type racer and E2A prototype, people were almost tearfully astonished by its winning combination of sensuality, technology and availability. In terms of culture, they commented on its erotic morphology: it seemed to predict the democratization of pleasure that was the keynote address of the Sixties. The design drew on Jaguar's backlist of glorious shapes, most particularly Malcolm Sayer's D-Type. This was a successful racing car designed by men in brown coats, a brilliant demonstration of the art and craft of penetration. A later Jaguar designer, Geoff Lawson, called it 'the optimum expression of steel'. Sayer and Lyons may have been influenced by Alfa Romeo's Disco Volante, but they achieved a unique synthesis. Anyway, great artists don't borrow, they steal. The design checklist: Stance, Proportion and Composition, Details and Symbolism. Elegant and aggressive, its phallic proportions amaze, but are moderated by the sober and balanced composition. Details have a feminine delicacy, although the beautiful faired-in glass headlamp lenses lasted only two years before they were legislated out of existence. The first production car in New York's Museum of Modern Art, it makes contemporary sculpture look ham-fisted. The 1961 Jaguar E-Type is proof, if proof were needed, that cars can be sublime works of art.

1961

BMW 1500

By the early Sixties, the German Wirtschaftswunder was a proven phenomenon and economic success brought a new sense of confidence in national characteristics. BMW now discovered the design language of the Bauhaus. Among the Neue Klasse series of 1961 were BMW's first truly modern cars, produced by a design team led by Wilhelm Hofmeister. There is a purity to the form of the 1500 and a precision in its details, a clarity in its structure, an implied hierarchy in the accumulation of meaningful details plus the suggestion of a strict, controlling intelligence that is, in its way, a complete expression of the prewar Bauhaus ideal. As Walter Gropius, the Bauhaus' founding director said, 'We aimed at realizing standards of excellence, not creating transient novelties.' Novelties included in the new 1500 established a template for BMW design over the next 40 years. Hofmeister had been educated at the Hamburg Wagenbauschule and brought an engineer's disciplines to the art of car design, first as Head of Body Engineering then as Chief Engineer. The 1500 has the BMW signature details which he authored: the prominent beltline, the big glasshouse and the reverse bend in the C-pillar – known as the Hofmeister-knick – which survived even Chris Bangle's radical assault on BMW design language in the early twenty-first century. A BMW 1500 painted in bone with tobacco leathertex upholstery, undecorated but supremely satisfying to the eye, is the perfect demonstration of Ludwig Mies van der Rohe's dictum: 'The Bauhaus was not an institution – it was an idea.' The Bauhaus was also a Neue Klasse BMW.

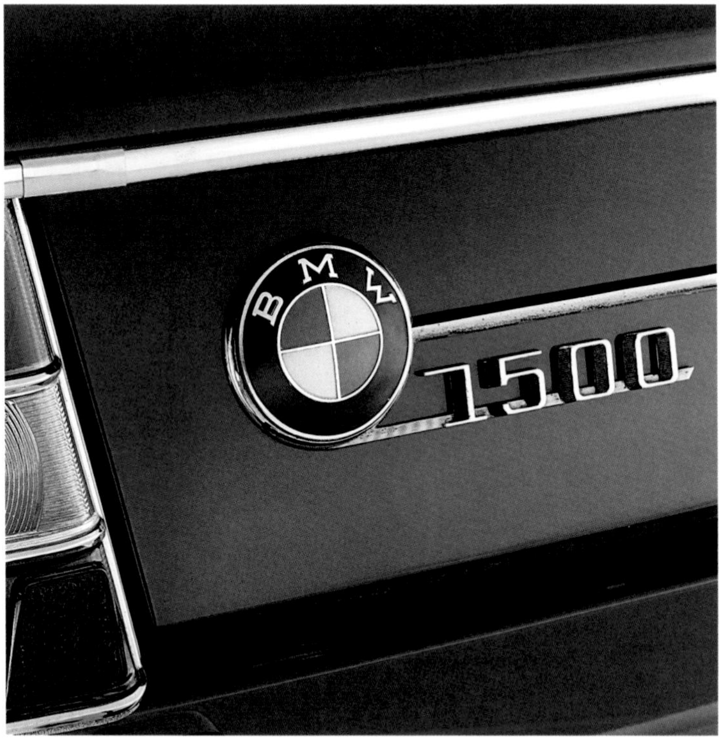
BMW
1500

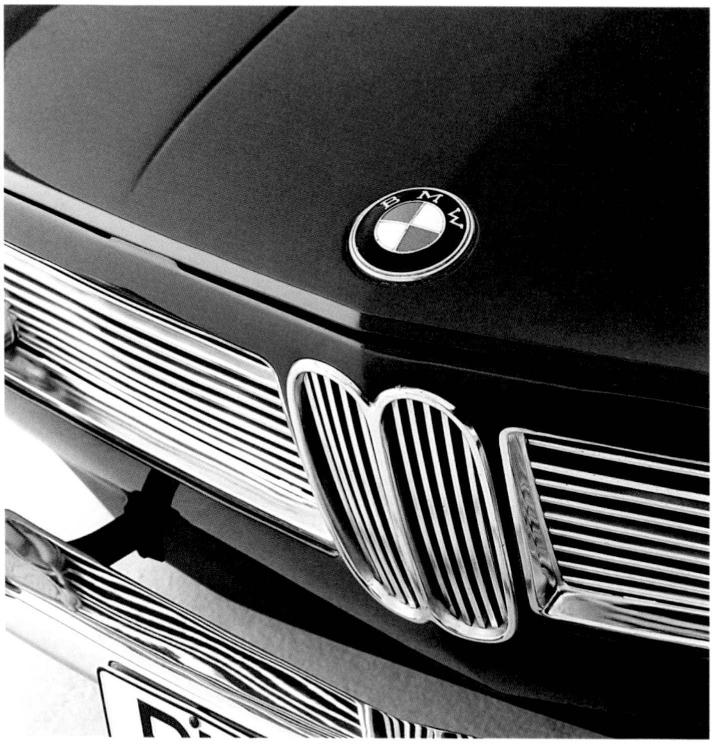
BMW

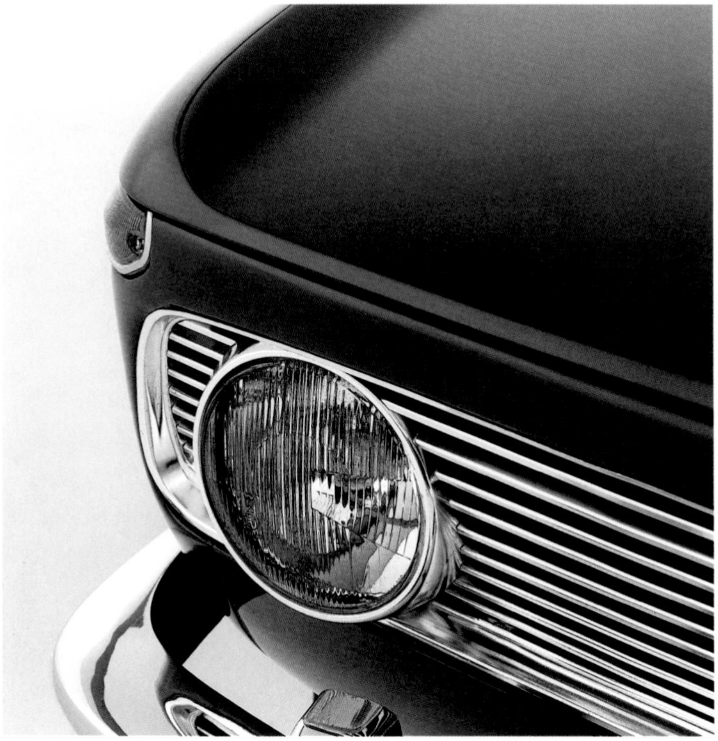

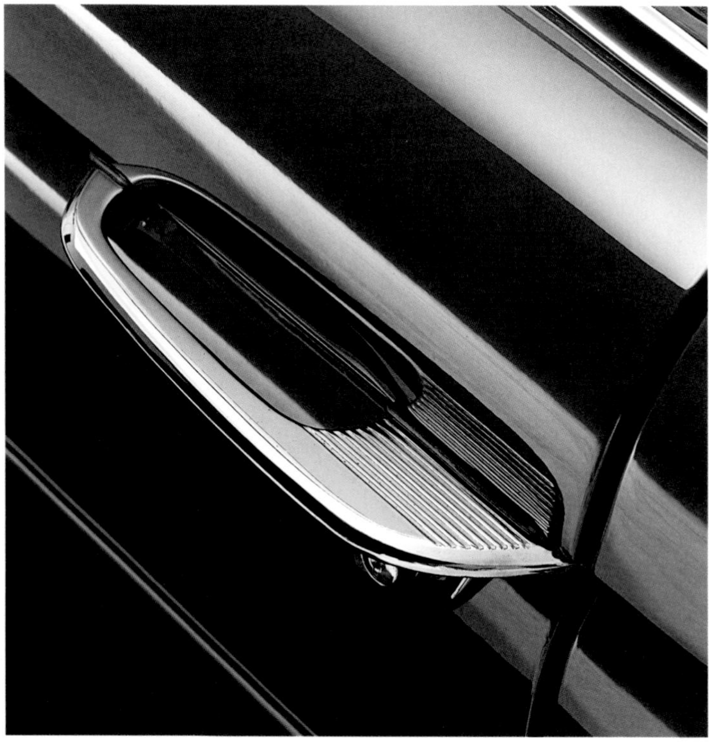

1961

NSU Prinz

Around the beginning of the twentieth century, a knitting-machine factory was established near the meeting of the rivers Neckar and Sulm in Germany – hence Neckarsulm – by Heinrich Stoll and Christian Schmidt. From knitting machines they soon progressed to motorbikes. By 1955, NSU was the world's largest manufacturer of them. Cars came later.

The 1961 Prinz was a subcompact, rear-engined four-seater, originally with a two-cylinder motor. It is remarkable in the history of car design since, as with the conflux of the Neckar and the Sulm, it represents a coming together of several significant influences. A background in the world of advanced German motorbikes gave NSU sophisticated technology, but it was an American business trip that gave the Prinz its unique appearance. An NSU board member returned from the US with cargo-cult memories of the Chevrolet Corvair, a landmark car drawn by Ned Nickles and 'Bud' Sugano. Like the Corvair, the Prinz had a distinctive flying-wedge roof with lip, a big glasshouse and an exaggeratedly prominent beltline that radically separated the upper and lower portions of the car. But unlike the Corvair, the Prinz had

this in a package of *Kleinwagen* proportions: it was a mere 3.43m (11 ft 3in) long, a jewel. Lightweight and compact high-performance engines made successive versions of the Prinz a pioneer of the compact sports saloon category which BMW later made its own, but when Volkswagen took over NSU in 1969 it was rapidly phased out, since management thought that its rear-engined format competed with the Beetle (which remained in production in Europe until 1978). This was ironic since in the mid-Thirties NSU had built some of the very first prototypes of Dr Porsche's Volkswagen. The Prinz was designed by Claus Luthe, who had been in the team responsible for the 1957 FIAT 500.

1961

Alfa Romeo Giulia

Alfa Romeo's Museo Storico in Arese near Milan has an example of the Tipo 103, an experimental small car that never went into production. But it carries most of the styling cues that made the Giulia one of Italy's most handsome modern cars. It is overtly '*tre volumi*' or three boxes: nose, cabin, boot. They said that it was 'designed by the wind', but it was actually designed along the aerodynamic precepts established by Dr Wunibald Kamm, the German wind-tunnel experimenter. The Giulia has a small frontal area, a curvaceous screen, body fluting that channels otherwise disruptive air, a tiny spoiler integrated into the trailing edge of the roof and a signature cut-off tail (or 'Kammheck'). To this distinctive general arrangement was added Alfa Romeo's handsome grille with attendant brightwork and *modernismo* twin headlights, together with an airy glasshouse. Although it gives an impression of being boxy, on further inspection the Giulia reveals itself to be a very subtle expression of the car designer's art. In fact, most edges are carefully radiused.

1961

Renault 4

The first advertisements for the R4 (known affectionately as '*La Quatrelle*') showed the car as a wire shopping basket with the caption 'Elle supermarche bien', confirming its utilitarian nature. Panels were flat and undecorated, the interior spartan, canvas seats on tubular frames could be removed. The R4 abandoned the rear-engined format of its predecessor (which had, curiously, been designed by Dr Porsche while in a French prison). Instead, its brilliant packaging was achieved by a compact engine sitting over the front axle. The first model sold in France was the R3, or *trois chevaux*: a deliberate suggestion that it was the successor to Citroën's ineffable two-horse-powered basket. Doggedly utilitarian, but charming, too, the R4 is an example of French design at its best: the unforced chic of the vernacular, as *typique* as a Duralex glass or a Bic pen. In this it was a successor to the notable range of French small cars that had been inspired by the postwar austerity legislation known as the Pons Plan. While the British Austin A40 in fact pioneered the hatchback format, the R4 (which sold 200,000 in its first year of production) made it popular. The *Quatrelle* had an agricultural aspect, but was in its way a fine shape. As the Russian journalist Iya Ehrenburg said, the French 'would put up with a feeble engine, but not ugly proportions'.

1962

Lancia Flavia Zagato

The *carrozzeria* of Ugo Zagato was founded in the Milanese suburb of Terrazzano di Rho in 1919. Early projects included rebodying undistinguished small FIATs in sporting aluminium. Light weight and motor sport became inspirations: Zagato built the bodywork of the magnificent Alfa-Romeo 158 and 159 which won the World Championship in the very first years of Formula One in 1950 and 1951. In road cars of the Fifties, Zagato began to use Plexiglass, a malleable material allowing the creation of sculpturally ambitious curves. Lancia introduced the polite, elegant Flavia saloon in 1960, a car whose expensive technical refinement contributed to the company's eventual bankruptcy. Zagato created a special-bodied Flavia known as the Sport in late 1962. It was designed by Ercole Spada, Zagato's in-house stylist who had joined the firm in 1960, aged 21. Spada had a wilful genius for emphatic, sometimes even uncomfortable, form. This is the most eccentric of Zagato's designs, developing the 'Panoramico Zagato' motif of the rear glass running into the roofline which was seen on show cars in the late Fifties. This rear-side glazing exploits roof space and gives passengers a unique panoramic and climatic experience: other manufacturers had experimented with similar devices, but only Lancia had the audacity to engineer opening windows. Early versions had the rear-wheel arch covered with integral spats, but this radical motif was dropped in the interests of practicality.

1963

Ford Cortina

The Ford Cortina has some claim to be the most successful British car of all, if not the most technologically adventurous or influential. It began as the Cardinal, a Detroit project for a subcompact which Lee Iacocca killed when he became the head of the Ford Division of FoMoCo in 1960. The Cortina was named after the Dolomites resort Cortina d'Ampezzo, home of the 1956 Winter Olympics. This was a gesture intended to confirm the supposed cosmopolitanism of its new ski-enthusiast class of customer. The first brochures for the Cortina included a graphic conceit showing rubber stamps from passport offices, again suggesting that Cortina owners were European travellers. Previous cars in the same social category had been named after tweedy and woolly university towns Oxford and Cambridge. Cortina was, on the other hand, for the plastics and nylon generation. There were other international influences, too. Designer Roy A. Brown had worked in Detroit

for George Walker on the calamitous Ford Edsel (research showed it failed because under hypnosis correspondents revealed its grille looked like a terrifying chrome vagina). As a punishment, he was sent to the Siberia of Ford's English plant at Dagenham in Essex. Out of this shaming humiliation there came the much-loved Cortina. Its secret, at a time when competitors were still offering cars whose interiors were modelled on country houses, was to offer a digestible dose of Americana to a generation just getting used to 77 Sunset Strip on the black-and-white telly. There was chrome, but not too much. Before the magic of America was devalued by calamitous military adventures, the Cortina offered a modest version of it for travelling salesmen. The poet John Betjeman understood its role in national life when he wrote, 'I am a young executive/No cuffs than mine are cleaner/I own a slimline briefcase/And I drive the firm's Cortina.'

1963

Porsche 911

This is the successor to the first Porsche, the 356. The body evolved from drawings made in the Fifties by Ferdinand-Alexander Porsche who later left the family firm to establish the independent Porsche Design. At the time, Butzi, as he was known to the family, was driving a Pontiac station wagon. 'In his day,' Butzi said of his grandfather, Dr Porsche, 'a designer did everything.' But by the time of the 911, a division of labour had had its effect, and Butzi Porsche acknowledged the infiltration of perfidious styling into the Holy Rites of engineering purity. 'Styling doesn't exist to provide new faces. It must strive for what is truly good.' The design is clearly based on Erwin Komenda's original Volkswagen and his Porsche 356. On 9 June 1960 the Porsche management sanctioned production of a six-cylinder engine for the 901. The production version was shown at Frankfurt in 1963. While clearly derived from the aesthetic of the 356, Butzi Porsche's design optimized the shape, making it longer and – at his father Ferry Porsche's insistence – capable of carrying a bag of golf clubs. While officially it was the Porsche Typ 901, Peugeot made legal claim to all three-digit denominations with a zero in the middle, so it became the 911. So great an esteem does the ultimate sport car enjoy that, even while there have been Porsche Typs 993, 996 and 997 since, they are all still known as the 911. Even after the New York atrocities of September 2001, Porsche saw no commercial reason to rename its masterpiece.

1963

Buick Riviera

The Buick Riviera was one of the ultimate 'personal' cars, the last gasp of American consumerism during Detroit's decadent Hellenistic period. The body was drawn in the General Motors Tech Center in Warren, Michigan (incongruously, a building designed by Finnish architect Eero Saarinen) by Ned Nickles. The Riviera (the name evokes Europhile longings felt in Michigan's country club belt) was the first great GM car after Harley Earl's retirement on 30 November 1959. The Riviera name had first appeared on a Buick Roadmaster in 1949, but England rather than France seems to have been the inspiration. Nickles' boss Bill Mitchell claimed to have been inspired by a Rolls-Royce seen in London one foggy night. The Riviera was conceived as a fully developed consumerized treat: so much so that the McCann Erickson ad agency did the design presentation to GM management. In the absence of any compellingly individual engineering philosophy, Buick depended to a special degree on the sort of desires stimulated by design and advertising. Often these were of an only faintly disguised erotic nature. In the Fifties Buick ran shameless advertisements with the copyline 'It makes you feel the man you are.' In the book *The Hidden Persuaders* (1957) Vance Packard revealed more of the occult sexual motivation. Buy a car that 'puts 12,000 pounds of thrust behind every engine stroke' he wrote. Or buy a car that's 'hot, handsome, a honey to handle'. That, for a very brief moment, was the gorgeously sculpted '63 Riviera.

1963

Rover P6

The Rover P6 is one of the greatest English saloon cars. While its predecessor, the stately P5, was much favoured by government officials and royalty, the P6 was directed at another market: the emergent executive class, a social and financial notch above the type satirized by John Betjeman, the ones who had been awarded 'the firm's Cortina'. Sold as the 2000, the name had an almost millennial ring. The designer was David Bache, son of Joe, an Aston Villa and England footballer. The younger Bache joined Austin in Birmingham in 1948 at the age of 23. Here he came under the influence of Italian designer Riccardo Burzi. Bache then joined Rover in 1954, participating in the P5 project. But the 2000 was a completely radical car, the most modern large car ever made in England. Originally designed to be powered by Rover's darling gas turbine engine, more conservative engines were tactfully employed. Like the Citroën DS, the 2000 had unstressed metal panels attached to a vast unitary frame. And like the DS,

its shape was totally original, with neither precedent nor successor. Unlike the DS, however, its design featured radical innovations in safety and ergonomics. Seat belts were standard for the sculpted front and rear bucket seats. Minor controls were logically arranged and switches were designed to break cleanly in an impact. An ingenious extension of the front headlamp lens refracted light, enabling drivers to pinpoint the nose accurately after dark. In daylight, Princess Grace of Monaco died at the wheel of a later V8-engined P6 (known as the 3500) when the car left the road near La Turbie on the Haute Corniche in the Riviera. A US specification P6 was featured in Austin Powers' film *The Spy Who Shagged Me*. The enormous promise of the P6, which combined Italianate elegance with good sense and sound engineering, was never fully realized because of the politicking morass that consumed the English car industry in the Seventies. Disenchanted, David Bache, one of the greatest car designers ever, left what remained of Rover in 1981.

1963

Mercedes-Benz SL

Paul Bracq was born in Bordeaux in 1933, trained in Paris' art school system and worked for industrial designer Philippe Charbonneaux, who specialized in car and truck design. In 1957 he joined the advanced design studios of Mercedes-Benz in Stuttgart, where one of his first projects was to work on the Model W113, launched as the 230SL in 1963. In Mercedes-Benz' language 'SL' stands for 'Super Leicht' (or Super Light). With an empty weight of 1,295kg (1.2 tonne), the SL was not emaciated, but Bracq created a design language whose unfussy, elegant linearity seemed to express concepts of lightness and athleticism, though – cleverly – not of insubstantiality, something which might have been ruinous to Mercedes-Benz' reputation for solidity. Viewed in side elevation, the SL is an arrangement of parallel lines. Viewed in frontal elevation, Bracq has made

emphatic use of the Mercedes-Benz star in a dramatically spare composition of air, metal and glass. But to view it as a whole is the most satisfactory way to look at an SL: it is a fine reconciliation of elegance and structural functionality. The signature 'pagoda' roof dips towards the middle and adds distinctiveness to distinction, but it was, in fact, a safety feature. The design of the SL betrays much influence from Bela Barenyi, Mercedes-Benz' Hungarian safety guru who filed 2,500 patents during his working life. One of them was in 1956 for the roof design, a feature that (as well as providing ease of access) enhanced structural rigidity and offered better passenger protection in the event of an unplanned vehicle inversion. In the Seventies Paul Bracq was one of the team of designers who created the French Train á Grande Vitesse.

1963

Chevrolet Corvette

The original Chevrolet Corvette appeared in 1953, an American attempt to come to terms with the English and Italian imports that had flooded the market after the creation of the Californian sports car cult of the late Forties. Harley Earl's original was produced in a run of only 300, but it was the first mass-produced car to use a fibreglass body. In everything except style the Corvette was a compromise (its lazy six-cylinder engine could scarcely turn its two-speed Powerglide transmission). But the style – which pioneered the wraparound windscreen in a production car – was sensational. Prototypes of its replacement began to appear in 1959; like the original, they were previewed in Motorama road shows. Innovations in the coupé in 1963 included hidden headlights, doors cut deeply into the roof, an aggressive profile and a distinctive split rear window. The dramatic whole was enhanced by glorious kitsch details including fake air vents and bogus knock-off wheels. The car looked like a diagram of desire. Design responsibility had now passed from Earl to his successor Bill Mitchell, who trained at the Barron Collier ad agency, joining GM Art and Color in 1935. Mitchell explained his creative philosophy: 'Pick up a billiard ball,' he once said, 'and it's boring. But pick up a baseball with all that texture and stitching and you play with it for hours.'

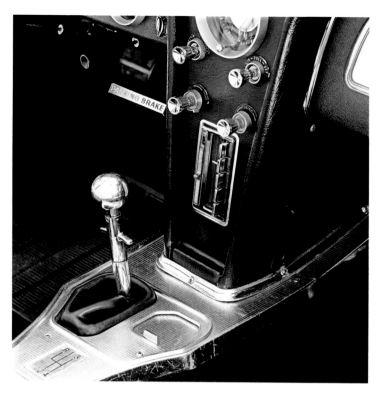

1963

Panhard 24CT

The Panhard 24CT is an elegiac car: the very last serious automobile produced by an independent French manufacturer. And, in this case, the manufacturer was the successor to Panhard et Levassor, one of the industry pioneers. A year after the 24CT went on sale in 1964, Panhard was sold to Citroën. In 1967 it produced its very last car, thereafter concentrating on military vehicles built for government contracts. The 24CT was the very opposite of a military vehicle: light, elegant, conceived with intelligent economy, but executed with a stylish *joie de vivre* and an intensely French suggestion that luxury can be enjoyed on any budget. Its mechanical layout followed well-established Panhard principles. There was a small, odd, flat twin engine, but it was nonetheless a large car. An efficient aerodynamic body (helped by experience of the Deutsch-Bonnet sports-racers which, using tough Panhard components, routinely won the Index of Thermal Efficiency at Le Mans) was an aid to curiously high performance. The 24CT was designed in-house and betrays many of the quirky idiosyncrasies that characterize French architecture and furniture design of the Sixties. There is an emphasis on horizontals and sometimes demanding angles, yet the

sense of sculptural form is unambiguous. The general arrangements can be traced back to the Panhard Dyna, but are here stretched, stylized, modernized. The interior, as individual as a French autoroute toll plaza, looks as though it might have been sketched by Olivier Mourgue. In the Thirties the 'L' for Emile Levassor was removed from the Panhard logo. However, almost as if in anticipation of the marque's extinction, the badge on the 24CT returned to the original prewar 'PL' design. The 24CT was not only the last Panhard, it was the very last time a manufacturer attempted a large, luxurious coupé conceived to be both fast and frugally efficient.

1963

Ferrari 250 GTO

This is the ultimate expression of the Ferrari idea. Enzo Ferrari said, 'I have never travelled anywhere as a tourist and have never had a holiday… for me the best holiday is going down to the factory.' The 250 GTO, an evolution of the 1959 250 GT, appeared at a press conference in February 1962. It was empirical aerodynamics, a version of its predecessor the 250 GT with a short wheel base, but optimized for racing. They modelled it in plaster of Paris over cloth. It was the evolution of a singular identity. Then Giotto Bizzarini went to the University of Pisa wind-tunnel. As a result, the car had a long, low snout, small radiator aperture, three evocative aerospace-style ducts, a rising tail, a fastback and an integrated spoiler. The 'passenger' had to contest space with the oil tank. Sergio Scaglietti was an inspired interpreter of Pininfarina's drawings, although in the case of this car it appears he used only the Pininfarina 'idea' of a Ferrari as a starting point. Enzo Ferrari himself was only concerned with racing – he said that he sold cars on Monday to pay his mechanics for working on a Sunday. It was Pininfarina's achievement to create a language that expressed this monomaniac devotion. Thirty-nine 'reproductions' of the original idea were built between 1962 and 1964, each one subtly different, the product of Sergio Scaglietti's hammer.

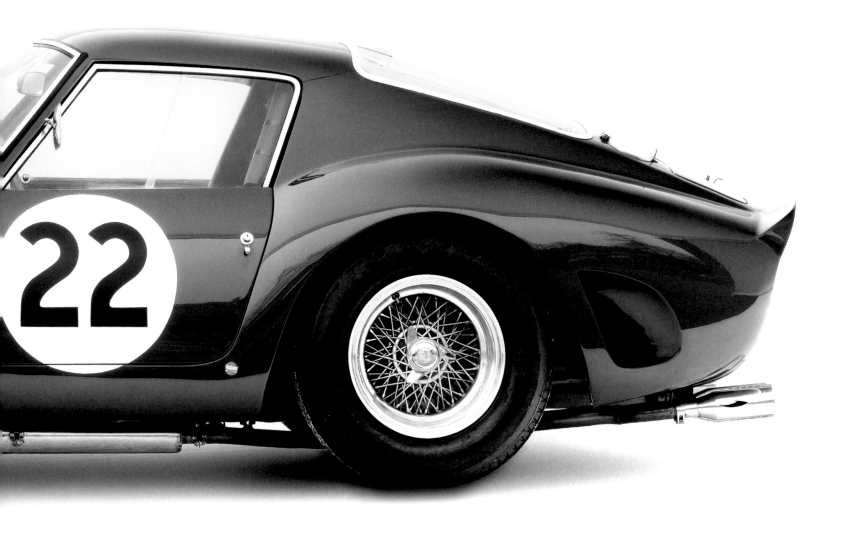

1964

Ford Mustang

The first drawings of the Mustang were made by John Najjar in January–February 1962, a response to a brief from Lee Iacocca formulated, the colourful myth has it, by Ford men and J. Walter Thompson men over steak and beer at Dearborn's Fairlane Inn. Target markets were defined as economy buyers, young performance buyers and affluent, middle-aged luxury buyers. In the end, everyone bought it. Success has many fathers, but failure is a bastard and many designers can claim authorship of the epochal Mustang, although perhaps Dave Ash and Joe Oros have ultimate claim to authorship. Eighteen clay models were made in the telescoped design process. Long hood, short deck, muscular aspect: the details were a catalogue of a nation's obsessions. 'The car to be designed by you,' the advertisements said. It was launched at New York's World's Fair on 13 April 1964, and Ford's restless and unscrupulous PR, Bob Hefty, sold it as an 'exclusive' cover story to both *Time* and *Newsweek*. The Mustang sold 518,000 in its first year. A Fastback version came in 1965. It was the ultimate consumer product: a brilliant slice of Americana, the Detroit equivalent of a Morris 1100. But it was defined by Madison Avenue: 'adjustable deep foam bucket seats… six color-keyed all-vinyl interiors… wall-to-wall carpeting… T-bar Cruise-o-Matic… Rally Pac'. It was a masterpiece of simulation, with racing stripes and accent paints.

Recite the options and it sounds like e. e. cummings. But it flattered to deceive, and had atrocious driving dynamics: the manual required the tyres to be inflated to 40psi if 'precision driving' was planned. The Mustang was also claimed as a triumph of marketing savvy, but Don Frey, a member of the original steak and beer gang, admitted to *Mustang Monthly* in 1983 that the claims about the car testing well in market research were a post hoc rationalization. It was originally to be called Torino, but as Henry Ford II was, at the time, squiring an Italian heiress, PR advised that this choice might backfire. The name Mustang was chosen by Jon Conley, the onomastic specialist at J. Walter Thompson.

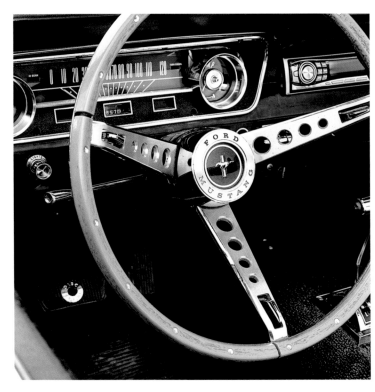

1964

Pontiac GTO

Designer Bill Porter was influenced by a number of sources. First, Harley Earl's 'highlight rule'. His dramatic profile for this remarkable car, including the emphatic Coca Cole bottle waist, makes the highlight run the entire length of this 2.92m (9ft 7in) wheelbase car. But Porter also cited de Kooning, Brancusi, the architecture of Frederick Kiesler and the furniture of Charles Eames. Porter's design method was based on 'surface development' disciplines of coachbuilding. He did four-view orthographic drawings, then he did sections and then the sections were turned into a 1:5 model by the application of clay. It was a mixture of nineteenth-century technical drawing and Renaissance sculpture. Real and apparent proportions played an important part in perceptions of the Pontiac, not least to alter the consumer's perceptions of a brand with a reputation for poor quality. An experimental independent rear suspension had allowed engineer John Z. De Lorean to see how low he could go (until this point Detroit's bodies had been getting absurdly wide, while the track remained narrow). Advertisements announced the 'Wide Track Look' and publicity drawings wildly exaggerated the proportions. This was the first moment in the history of art when width became sexy. Then De Lorean, who liked European sports cars, decided to insert a vast 5,178 cubic cm (316 cubic in) V-8 into the Tempest. The result was the preposterously fast GTO, named shamelessly after the Ferrari Gran Turismo Omologato. This was the start of the muscle-car craze. The Pontiac agency had Ronnie and the Daytonas, a cargo-cult Beach Boys, record 'Little GTO'.This hot-rod classic ('turn it on, wind it up, blow it out') went gold in 1964. The Pontiac GTO cost $3,200, but De Lorean himself said, 'If America's teenagers couldn't afford a GTO that day, the success of the car meant they were going to think Pontiac first when they could.'

1965

Toyota 2000GT

This, with the later Datsun 240Z, was a Japanese response to the Jaguar E-Type, which it closely resembles in proportion and general arrangement, if not in details. A source of both cars was early work by Albrecht Goertz for Yamaha, who eventually manufactured the sophisticated cylinder heads used on the truck engine used in the production version of this car. However, very few were actually made: just 337, including two used by the cinema version of James Bond in an early and influential example of product placement. It is, thus, that rarest of things: a limited edition Japanese product. The 2000GT was, at a time when Toyota was trying to establish itself in Western markets, evidence of the increasing confidence of the Japanese motor industry, although its design was wholly derivative of European and American originals. Details include aero mirrors and a racing-style fuel cap (although at this time Toyota had no real record of competition success yet) and cute service doors, suggestive of deep, satisfying covert technology. The striking phallic morphology spoke an international language, although in the chrome, jewellery and bizarrely shaped orifices an original Japanese formal language is beginning to emerge.

1966

Oldsmobile Toronado

Errett Lobban Cord made the first giant American cars with front-wheel drive. Oldsmobile made the last. In fact, the 1966 Oldsmobile Toronado was the last great US car, irrespective of the traction system: the editors of *Consumer Guide* called it a 'landmark creation', but it is really more of a tombstone, a memorial to that slide from grace described by Brock Yates in his 1984 book *The Decline and Fall of the American Automobile Industry*. The '66 Toronado (the name is a splendid example of General Motors' bizarre habit of mangling perfectly good words) began as 1962 sketches for a dream car known as 'The Red Renderings' by Oldsmobile's Assistant Chief Designer, David North… although the car should properly be seen as the last, ultimate, final expression of the aesthetic adventure begun in 1927 by Harley Earl and completed in 1966 by his successor as design boss, Bill Mitchell. Toronado is a superlatively transgressive technical concept, tightly wrapped in fuss-free sculpture of complete originality. The compact front-wheel-drive system did not seduce Oldsmobile into making a compact package: the Toronado had a wheel base of nearly 3m (10ft , or the length of a Mini) and weighed 1,980kg (4,366lb). Yates explains that Oldsmobile engineers evaluated an E-Type, a Corvette, a Ferrari and a racing Porsche 904, but did not understand these cars and had them lurching around at 32kp/h (20mph) in fifth gear, complaining about the noisy Jaguar and cramped Chevy. So they did something original instead. The styling is bold and simple: massively flared wheel arches create a motif in their own right and the C-posts of the pillarless coupé glide lasciviously into a fastback. Toronado was the last 'personal' car: soon afterwards US manufacturers lost their confidence in vulgar magnificence.

1966

Toyota Corolla

Plain of aspect and technologically unadventurous, the Toyota Corolla is the most successful car ever made. The perfect product of the Japanese industrial method (which has been called 'the machine that changed the world'), the 1966 Corolla is a demonstration of what can be achieved by the teamwork of subordinated egos instead of the bravura imaginings of the autonomous genius. It suggests an alternative definition of 'design'. From the day it was founded in 1931 by Kiichiro Toyoda, Toyota was committed to self-sufficiency. Accordingly, it established rigid disciplines and methodologies. As a result, while in 1956 annual Toyota production had been about 12,000 units, by 1970 it was comfortably over a million… most of them Corollas. The name 'Corolla' was first used in 1961 on one of Toyota's five domestic sales channels, established to sell a car called Publica. The sales channel and the car became the Corolla when the Publica name was dropped in 1966. At Toyota the sales channel team was directly involved with the factory's product planning, and sales and engineering staff were continuously being churned. At the Corolla University, students were taught marketing. In the showroom mornings began with a team meeting followed by door-to-door sales. Corolla people learnt demographics and

metrics. And for aesthetic inspiration (to save time and money), they looked to America – where the Corolla was introduced in 1968. In design terms it was an American car in miniature: chrome, white walls, shiny vinyl, a variety of body styles. The Sprinter coupé may even have looked like a miniature Mustang, but at about 725kg (1,600lb) it weighed not much more than half as much. As Sony did with transistors, Corolla fed America back to itself. At a time when Ralph Nader had crystallized native American disenchantment with its favourite product, the consumer's experience of Corolla (especially as a pitilessly abused car rental) offered a reliable alternative. For patriots, this was made palatable when Corolla became the first Japanese car to be manufactured in the United States.

1966

Volvo 144

There is a fantastic pathos about this car which seems to map the coordinates of Swedish design. The mid-Sixties, when it was launched, was the last moment of innocence for the influential Swedish design movement before the global success of IKEA turned social-democratic aesthetics into a tacky marketing phenomenon. Jan Wilsgaard began the design process in 1960, responding to an unrealistically demanding management brief. By 1964, the general arrangements of the car had been confirmed. Production cars were shown to the press in August 1966. The 144 carried established Volvo styling cues, including the nostrils first seen on Wilsgaard's Amazon, but they are here reduced to vestigial motifs in the radiator brightwork. Wilsgaard's nostrum 'Simple is beautiful' (which pays homage to early twentieth-century Swedish design philosophy) may not be fully proven here, but the architecture of the 144 has a dignity and clarity that allowed the car to become a development platform for more than 20 years. It was the 144 that was Volvo's basis for the increasingly significant

semantics of safety which, eventually, it turned into a house style. From simple rubber guard strip inserted into the bumpers, by the time of the last models the 144 had acquired enormous protective apparatus front and rear. Other devices, including the energy-absorbing reverse slant nose, trialled on Experimental Safety Vehicle concepts of the Seventies, first went to market on the 144. This was the last pure Volvo before globalization, takeovers, mergers and misjudged alliances compromised the company's once essentially Swedish spirit.

1966

Alfa Romeo Duetto Spider

In the *Lessico della carrozzeria* (1979), Pininfarina defines 'Spider' as 'La vettura sportive per eccelenza, generalamenta a 2 posti, con carrozzeria aperta e capote ripiegabile'. ('The sports car par excellence, generally two seats with open bodywork and a folding hood.') The Alfa Spider was the company's first modern two-seater in the same way that the Ford Transit, introduced the same year, was Ford's first modern van. To publicize it Alfa held an international competition to find a name. The winner was a Signor Guidobaldo Trionfi of Brescia with 'Duetto'. It was a modern coinage, but the factory soon reverted to tradition. In May 1966 the first batch of Duettos was exported to the United States and the following year the car entered global folk memory when it was Dustin Hoffman's transport in Mike Nichols' *The Graduate*, a film that closed the generation gap with its slickly packaged and elegantly photographed transgressive or, at least, transgenerational, sex. The design was by Pininfarina, with reflections of earlier experimental Alfas, especially the Disco Volante (or Flying Saucer) of 1955. The Duetto's tail was originally an elegant, curvaceous boatback or what the Italians call a '*coda di rospo*' (cuttlefish tail). This was changed in 1970 to a truncated rear, vaguely suggestive of the aerodynamic 'Kammheck', the sharply cut-off treatment advocated by Wunibald Kamm, wizard of aerodynamics. Not a lot about the Duetto was quite so scientific.

1967

NSU Ro80

In 1990 Claus Luthe, who had been in the design team working on the FIAT Cinquecento, was imprisoned for murdering his drug-addict son. Earlier, he had designed the body of the most radically engineered production car ever. Development began in 1961 and it was launched at the Frankfurt Motor Show six years later: to avoid nagging questions of personal vanity, no design or engineering credits were given. So rumours began that this dramatic shape had been sculpted by Giacomo Manzu. Luthe, in his own words, aimed at 'sleekness and elegance'. The compact Wankel rotary engine allowed the dramatic wedge shape, although Luthe's most radical ideas were compromised by production realities. Early proposals included versions with sliding doors. For instance, the front wheel arch looks too big for the tyre because at the last minute engineers insisted on changing the springs without allowing the designer to alter the radius of the arch. Engineers also altered the width of the car, compromising the purity of the designer's original idea. The Ro80 was intuitively aerodynamic: it first went into a wind-tunnel after the design was complete. The roof was intended to be brushed stainless steel, giving the glasshouse an appearance of immateriality. Razor edges '*Abrisskanten*' were combined with a K-heck (for Kamm tail): advertisements said '*Avantgardismus*'. In April 1977 the last car left the Neckarsulm factory and the name NSU died.

1967

Alfa Romeo Montreal

Alfa Romeo, then a state-owned company, was asked to contribute an exhibit to the Expo '67 in Montreal, a world's fair that also launched Israeli architect Moshe Safdie's 'Habitat'. In Montreal the Alfa Romeo was a centrepiece of the 'Man-the-maker' exhibit, although organizers may have been unaware of the car's functional and ergonomic shortcomings.

In terms of cultural reference, the astonishing Montreal was conceived in the year Sergeant Pepper was published; in terms of style, it is midway between the fashion eccentricities of Paco Rabanne (who thought women should wear frocks of plastic and aluminium) and the coming age of the first-generation pocket calculators. For the Montreal, Alfa adapted the V-8 engine of the successful T33 sports racing car, but mounted it in the front, giving the futuristic car a primeval phallomorphic profile. Despite its intergalactic allure, the rest of the Montreal was based on the humdrum 1750 saloon. Creative credits went to engineers Orazio Satta Puliga and Giuseppe Busso. Design credits went to Bertone as a whole, but specifically to his two *enfants terribles*, Giorgetto Giugiaro and

Marcello Gandini, rivals for his crown. The Montreal, all voluptuous curves, evocative metal, slats and Plexiglass lenses, beautiful proportions and odd colours, was clearly – especially from the rear – inspired by Giugiaro's 1966 Miura for Lamborghini (which, while the maestro prefers the FIAT Panda, most would regard as his masterpiece). The significance of the Montreal is as an attempt, on a budget, to commercialize the most extreme fantasies of the car designer. They said it was 'la sportive di classe che parla al futuro', but really it is evocative of an innocent age whose dreams never came to pass. A fine period photograph shows the Montreal show cars being loaded on to a vintage BEA freighter for its transatlantic journey. The production version of the Montreal was released at the 1970 Salon de l'Automobile in Geneva. The advertisements said that it was a 'dream car come true'. On this occasion they were wrong. While consumer response to the show cars was near-hysterical, the Alfa Romeo reality failed to match the Alfa Romeo imagination and production ended in 1975 with fewer than 4,000 Montreals built.

1968

Ferrari Daytona

At a lunch meeting in Tortona in 1951, Enzo Ferrari declared his disappointment with the image of his cars, since they were being bodied by different coachbuilders. His lunch companion, Battista 'Pinin' Farina (accompanied by his son Sergio) now took responsibility. A quarter of a century later, a Ferrari design language had been clearly established and the 365/GTB4, as it is correctly known, was its ultimate expression. The Daytona was named, with an eye to the American market, after a famous victory in the 24-hour race at the Daytona Speedway in Florida in 1967 when three Ferrari sports-racers crossed the line abreast. There is an American self-consciousness about the car. Although it is based on the harsher and more rudimentary GTB/4, the Daytona was bigger and softer. Significantly, most cars retained the signature wheels of the successful sports-racers: five-spoke alloy castings in a distinctive star pattern, usually painted gold. This is not the purest Ferrari, but it is one of the most significant. It is a Ferrari conceived not as racing car but a luxury product and it has styling to match. There are two unusual expressive elements: the concave side-moulding and the aero-nose which marked the (temporary) formal subjugation of the Ferrari frontal orifice. (This nose detail was later copied by David Bache in the 1975 Rover SD1.)

The Daytona was the last front-engined Berlinetta and the last Ferrari to be produced on the old studio/workshop system; Pininfarina would send a prototype to the Ferrari factory at Maranello. This would be reviewed by Ferrari himself, as well as by his dealers. After critical comments had been made and agreed, the car was handed over to master metal-basher Sergio Scaglietti who, in the words of Valerio Moretti, himself 'possessed the technical abilities and creative insight of a great designer'. Scaglietti would then make a limited edition of 'reproductions' of the original. In the early Seventies the Ferrari factory withdrew from sports-car racing and a vital connection to a creative source was lost. The Daytona was the last of its type.

1968

Jaguar XJ6

The XJ (for 'Experimental Jaguar') was the last car in which the handwriting of Sir William Lyons, the company's quixotic founder, can unambiguously be seen. Regularly cited as one of the most beautiful four-door cars ever made, it was the last true Jaguar before the ugly miscegenations and brawls of failed industrial marriages compromised a unique spirit. The XJ4 programme began in 1964. First proposals included a very Italianate car. There were some pleasing detail minutiae: smaller twin symmetrical fuel tanks allowed the creation of a functional square boot and Dunlop's new low-profile tyres allowed the production XJ6 to make the most of the exceptional stance required by its exquisitely realized body. It was a modern car, although there were fine period details: the signature eyelids over the two pairs of headlamps were a gorgeous and complex sculptural detail that conferred great character on the car, but they were not optimized for automated production and required an uneconomical number of processes to finish. As soon as new owners sought 'value engineering' (a euphemism for 'cost-cutting') they were rationalized away. The XJ6 had a notably thin-pillared glasshouse and pronounced tumblehome. The rising hipline just forward of the rear wheel arch is much too subtle to be compared with the vulgarian 'Coca-Cola bottle curve' of contemporary Chevrolets and Pontiacs, instead conferring on the car something of the animal grace of its feral namesake.

1970

Citroën SM

The bizarre Citroën SM had a unique frontal aspect as well as a number of other unique aspects, many of them less happily resolved. It remains one of the most extremely odd cars to have gone into production. Conceived as the (illogical) development of the 1955 DS, the SM achieved more notoriety than celebrity. Notoriety because the creative ambition of its manufacturers so far exceeded their practical abilities. The number plate behind glass is a defining detail that was borrowed from a prototype of Claus Luthe's NSU Ro80, spied when Citroën and NSU were collaborating on the Comotor project to share the technology of the Wankel rotary engine. This had its origins in Citroën's historic dissatisfaction at never having fitted the old Goddess with an engine as fine as the rest of the car. But the Wankel engine's shortcomings perplexed even the saintly, and the strange SM was the product of another and even more unlikely collaboration… with Maserati (which Citroën had, somewhat idiosyncratically, acquired in 1968). SM in fact stands for 'Serie Maserati'. Curious details include asymmetric seating and the

world's first injection-moulded GRP (glass reinforced plastic) wheels. The lascivious body, a four-seat coupé apparently modelled on a fantastical Gallic spaceship, was drawn by Robert Opron and built by specialists Henri Chapron. Compared with a contemporary Aston Martin, the SM appears a miracle of integrated shapemaking. While a Seventies Aston Martin is all difficult angles and two dimensions, the SM is magnificently sculpted: the total expression of a unique formal idea. A four-door convertible was built for Le Président. Graham Greene drove one. Despite this celebrity endorsement and the sense of awe and wonder this remarkable car generated everywhere it was seen, crippling production and reliability problems fatally compromised the consumers' experience and production stopped in 1975. The designer, Robert Opron, subsequently disappeared. The tailgate window of the SM contained the largest and most complicated piece of automotive glass made up to that time. The glass covering the front lamps was so difficult to manufacture that it is said about a quarter of production had to be discarded.

1970

Range Rover

Consumers of 1970 were used to wheel trims and whitewalls, or fake exhaust pipes. Then, on Wednesday 17 June, something else was offered: a car that was like nothing before or since, a superior exercise in advanced product design wedded to British pragmatism. The first customers may have been bewildered Welsh sheep farmers, but that soon changed. People realized they were not being sold a four-wheel-drive utility vehicle. They were being sold an aesthetic absolute. In the Range Rover British good manners were introduced to the type of vehicle normally in the hands of an American genre of Coors-chugging grunt. The Range Rover made utility chic; a piece of agricultural equipment was consumerized into an attractive package. The Range Rover put form on what had hitherto been indeterminate. The car had rational and intelligent details, balanced, in emotional terms, between assertive and gentlemanly. Its origins were in a Fifties concept of 'Road Rover', a hybrid agricultural vehicle and saloon car, but Range Rover went further: a perfect psychographic representation of the aspirations of the market sector it established. Later, like all good designs, it showed itself capable of development and turned into various mutations. Engineers Spen King and Gordon Bashford with designer David Bache began work on the Range Rover in 1967. They ignored an axiom and produced a design that did not take time to acquire brand values, but had them from the start. Signature design features included a roof that appears to float above black-painted pillars, a calm shell bonnet and 'castellations' which offered the driver an automotive version of a weapon's sights. It was functionality turned into design language. And then there was a mass of features, smaller than the architecture, that had a profound effect on the customer's perceptions of this exciting new product. Interior details were elegantly modern and conceived to be modular. There was a hose-down plastic interior. Originally, the concept was felt to be so correct, that there was a single model with a single specification. The 1970 Range Rover established a new product type conforming to Goethe's definition of genius: putting form on what was hitherto indeterminate.

1971

Alfasud

Alfasud began in 1968, a project by the then state-owned Alfa Romeo to have a car suitable for production in the Mezzogiorno, the troubled south of the country with criminal and agricultural rather than industrial and manufacturing traditions. The engineer responsible for the Alfasud was Rudolf Hruska, a one-time collaborator with Ferdinand Porsche. But his concern here was packaging. Space utilization was exceptional: of an overall 3.96m (13ft) length, 2.8m (9ft 2in) are for passengers and luggage. His boxer engine has clear Porsche heredity, but allows a short and low nose. It was placed ahead of the front axle so the interior is not compromised by any intrusions. Giorgetto Giugiaro of ItalDesign in Moncalieri, near Turin, was commissioned to design the body. It was his first mass-market project. Hruska presented a tight dimensional brief and the demand for high visibility meant a low beltline and large glasshouse were inevitable. Doors make maximum possible use of the space between the wheels. Giugiaro placed the windscreen well forward, an effect that emphasizes the large passenger cell. At the rear a fastback descends to a vertical tail. The Alfasud had an exceptionally low drag coefficient of 0.30.

1971

FIAT 130 Coupé

This car was the result of an aesthetic experiment begun when Pininfarina showed its Florida II concept in 1957. While based on Lancia components, Pininfarina's Florida II established the artistic standards for large European cars for the next quarter-century. Its rear doors hinged at the trailing edge (providing excellent access) were not imitated, but its handsome, almost severe, lines and aristocratic stance were much copied, if never bettered. There may be no such car as a 'Pininfarina', but the big FIAT coupé of 1972 comes close. This was a version of the FIAT 130, a premium-priced large car that was an (in the event misplaced) expression of confidence by a company that made its reputation out of economy and moderation. The saloon was designed by FIAT's in-house Centro Stile. And Giacosa directed his team not to ape the timelessness of Mercedes-Benz, but to aim for effects a little more American in character. He always had misgivings, since his heart was in the design of small cars with all the interesting disciplines of intellectual economy and material parsimony a modest budget imposed. As a result, the 1969 130 saloon was not well born. The design of the Coupé was given to Pininfarina and the car appeared at the 1972 Geneva Salon. Confidently undecorated, razor-edged, imposing, glassy and elegant, it was the final expression of one Italian tradition. Later that year, an exhibition at New York's Museum of Modern Art called 'Italy: The New Domestic Landscape' set a new schema for Italian design and set the agenda for a new generation who had a decided antipathy to the car.

Lamborghini Countach

The plan view of a Lamborghini Countach makes it clear that it is, conceptually speaking, an origami graphic of other-worldly outrage, although it is not made of Japanese paper, but of aircraft-grade aluminium. The prototype, known as Project 112, was shown at the Geneva Salon de l'Automobile in 1971. The 10-year gap since the Jaguar E-Type appeared there allowed the public to accumulate reserves of astonishment, all spent on viewing this astonishing car. The Countach was designed by Marcello Gandini, who took the seat left empty at Carrozzeria Bertone when Giorgetto Giugiaro set up on his own in 1965. Gandini's style combines aggressive angularity and dramatic proportions with a sublime refusal to consider practicalities. The Countach's signature scissor doors were required because conventional openings were not practicable on this imponderably wide car. Challenges to functionality included negligible rear vision, not much aided by a periscope rear-view mirror. The passenger cab is placed very well forward and inside there are period-style digital instruments. The car is only 1m (3ft 6in) tall. 'Countach' is Piedmontese *voce de gergo*, the gasp of astonishment made , for example, on sight of an exceptionally attractive woman. The car was manufactured from 1974 to 1990 and established the category of 'supercar'. Supercars belong to a specific moment in history, as if willed into existence by a collective need. There have always been automobiles of extreme performance and appearance, but the emergence of an identifiable group with observable co-variations in type and behaviour that an industrial anthropologist would recognize belongs to the late Sixties and early Seventies. Just as this period saw the invention and separation of powerful and charismatic supergroups from the swill of ordinary pop, so the supercar became a type when the mass market had been satisfied by waves of ingenious small front-wheel-drives. After so much low-brow consumer satisfaction, extreme stimuli were needed at the other end of the market. The Countach is the definitive supercar: a shape so dramatic that it still astonishes more than 35 years later. Supercars might be ridiculous… but they are never boring.

Supercar: [origin obscure] *From 'super' (Latin) above, on top of, beyond, besides, an excess of; and 'car' (Medieval Eng.), a wagon. A private passenger vehicle, usually Italian, often of lascivious and outrageous appearance with astonishing proportions. Generally carrying only two people, characterized by extreme performance, inflammatory rejection of secondary ergonomics and total disregard for basic functionality. A virtue made of extravagance and inconvenience.*

1972

BMW 5 Series

1972 was the year of the Olympics in Munich, BMW's sacred site. In fact, the Olympic Stadium was built on the old Flugplatz where BMW had begun making aero-engines in 1917. It was a moment of optimism for both Germany and BMW. The country was now fully confident since the democratic and economic benefits of the Wirtschaftswunder had, at least partially, compensated for earlier horrors. At the Olympics the graphic designer Otl Aicher (also a consultant to BMW) had created a new world standard of signage with a precision and clarity that said 'Germany'. For its own part, BMW built a Hochhaus, a headquarters building, inspired by the shape of an internal combustion engine. It is known as the Vierzylinder (four cylinder). Next to it, in a huge arena inspired by Frank Lloyd Wright's Guggenheim Museum in New York, is BMW-Welt, a theatre where corporate values were put on the stage. The 1972 5 Series was the protagonist. The designer was Frenchman Paul Bracq, who had earlier worked on the Mercedes-Benz 300SL, and would later work on Alstom's Train à Grande Vitesse for the Société Nationale des Chemins de Fer.

He became Design Director of BMW in 1970. For the new Fünfer, Bracq took the design language established by Willhelm Hofmeister, but adapted it to a contemporary package: twin headlights in a full-width black grille, crisp graphics with a prominent beltline, emphatic jewellery, a masculine stance with feminine details and radii. And then there was a big glasshouse. A German critic complained, 'Why should a car have so much glass?', explaining that glass is heavier, more expensive and more dangerous than metal. But the critic was ignored. The success of the Fünfer showed that consumer choices are emotional, not rational. The 5 Series offered a synecdoche of middle-class values, setting a design standard that was effectively unaltered for a quarter of a century.

1972

Renault 5

Although the word did not exist at the time, this was the first modern hatchback. The Renault 5, although based on the very dated running gear of the R4, was a radical innovation in car architecture: to a package as neat as the Mini, it added French style, a hatchback and the signature polyester wraparound bumpers (a world first). It was designed by Michel Boué who died, aged 35, before the car's commercial debut in 1972. While the British Mini had utilitarian charm, the French R5 had urban chic. Boué's sculpture was wholly original: there were large areas of shockingly plain metal and generous glazing. An uncompromisingly plain nose and a preponderance of vertical and near-vertical lines gave the car an attractively alert aspect. There were some notably architectural details, too: handles were cleverly integrated into the trailing edge of the door and the interior was frankly addressed to an audience not yet debauched by the fripperies of postmodernism: it was stark, but clever. Originally Boué proposed rear lights running the entire length of the C-pillar. This motif, which later became an industry cliché, was rejected on grounds of cost. Media promotion was intense and the car embarrassingly anthropomorphized in advertisements shown in 268 Paris and 1,446 provincial cinemas, where it appeared as a cute person. The Publicis advertising agency directed communications towards women, students and other '*étrangers*'. Whether or not the delightful R5 threatened conventional French conceptions of masculinity, it immediately took 5.8 per cent of the French market.

1974

Volkswagen Golf

The success of Dr Porsche's Volkswagen almost ruined the company. As late as 1970 it was still the company's single most important product. It sold well, but was pitiably *retardataire* compared with the best from European and – increasingly – Japanese manufacturers. Five thousand Beetles were made a day, but this was as embarrassing as Ford building Model Ts in the mid-Seventies. It was a poor advertisement for a culture of technocrats. The Golf was the eventual result of management wranglings and procrastination: a late-flowering commitment to modernism and to new technology. It was a German take on Alec Issigonis' Mini formula, but executed with more precision and harder edges. Significantly, the body was based on designs not made by a Wolfsburg lab technician, but by the great Giorgetto Giugiaro. As soon as he made himself independent of Bertone, Giugiaro set up ItalDesign. Its first car was the Alfasud, its second the Golf, one of the most significant cars of all time. The Golf is almost entirely comprised of straight lines and flat panels, but the effect was not one of tectonic crudeness, rather of breathtaking novelty. These shallow panels simplified the manufacturing process and there was a concomitant restraint in details. In fact, early Golfs were astonishingly minimal: drivers sat upright on hard, vertical seats with very few concessions to comfort, let alone luxury. Instruments were in a single pod and inside was hard, shiny plastic. With his insistence on linearity and clarity, Giugiaro helped Volkswagen to create an intensely desirable product. Its generous glass areas added daylight to a thrilling sense of freshness. The Golf's style was criticized by some as ham-fisted industrial origami, but it is a sharp-edged box of great subtlety. More significantly, while the straight lines and flat panels were an expression of Giugiaro's aesthetic at the time, it also served notice that Volkswagen was reborn: the Beetle's period curves and radii were emphatically replaced by modern linear geometry. American Golfs were called Rabbits and made in an abandoned Chrysler factory in Pennsylvania. Like all excellent designs, the Golf is capable of development: five model cycles have not departed from the original proposition.

1977

SAAB 99 Turbo

The SAAB 99 was introduced in 1969, the company's second only product line. Drawings from the mid-Fifties by designer Sixten Sason predict the general arrangement of the 99: a truncated tail, a nose-down attitude and a big glasshouse with low waistline. One version shows dramatic glazing, a feature which continued into production: SAAB 99s are unique in having a windscreen that is almost semi-circular in plan. A running prototype in the SAAB Museum in Trollhattan built in the mid-Sixties (when the design was established) shows how SAAB's thinking was evolving: the car was to be a big Swedish Mini. Sason was assisted in the studio by an English architect, Peter Maddock, and his protégé, Bjorn Envall. It was Envall who led the team that turned the humdrum 99 into the 1977 Turbo. BMW produced a limited edition Turbo 2002 in 1973, but the SAAB Turbo established a new product category. And Bjorn Envall gave it a design language. The original two-door 99 was turned into a more interesting hatchback called the 900. Envall wanted to achieve stand-out for a new, fast, technologically interesting car. He put a spoiler underneath the rear window. He designed alloy wheels that created a stroboscopic effect on the move. Most cars were specified in dramatic and sinister black paint. Envall made vents and jewellery emphatic. The 99 Turbo revolutionized the consumer's perception of SAAB; it was no longer a Swedish curiosity but a badge of honour among affluent sophisticates everywhere. When the Police Department of Aspen, Colorado, decided it had to buy an intelligent foreign car on environmental grounds, it chose SAAB.

1979

FIAT Panda

In the late Seventies FIAT enhanced its corporate image after a period of lacklustre products with the Ritmo, whose advertisements declared it to be 'handmade by robots'. The ads won more awards than the car, even if it could boast body design by Bertone (the firm's last for a significant mass-market car). The Panda was the second front of this offensive. It was not just designed by an external consultancy, but worked up to a fully engineered package ready for manufacture. The consultancy was ItalDesign, founded by Giorgetto Giugiaro, the greatest Italian car designer after Pininfarina. Giugiaro had made his name at Bertone (where he was an influential *éminence grise*) then with the autograph Alfasud and Volkswagen Golf. In offering not just agreeable body design, but an entire viable package, Giugiaro distanced himself from the old *carrozzerie*. His opportunity with the Panda was to establish himself as the most innovative, yet practical, designer. Conceived as a successor to the original FIAT Zero-A and its descendant, the adorable Cinquecento, with the Panda Giugiaro wanted to make an intelligent utilitarianism chic. He broke strict industry taboos and made a virtue of asymmetry with its off-centre air intake. He wanted to make economy explicit and used flat glass (which by the Law of Unintended Consequences actually made production more expensive). Proportioned to fit into narrow alleys in Italian hill towns, the Panda was given boldly expressive polypropylene impact protection that occupied nearly a third of the car's surface area. Metal panels were uncomplicated pressings. Inside, the modular instrument panel could be quickly adapted to either left- or right-hand drive. There was enormous internal storage space and a striking simplicity. Like the Citroën deux chevaux which it conceptually resembles, hammock-type seats could be removed and there was a single windscreen wiper. The Panda was the first car to be more of a product design than an automobile and established Giugiaro as the pre-eminent consultant designer. For his part, he said that it was his most complete design.

1982

Ford Sierra

Finding a successor to the famous and successful Cortina tested Ford's marketing genius and its nerve. On the one hand, by the early Eighties it was necessary to offer a more sophisticated design to compete with Japanese imports (the Sierra was officially a part of Ford's 'AJ' or 'After Japan' programme), but at the same time it was dangerous to alienate Ford's conservative customers. With ideas about aerodynamics and safety influencing the auto industry's designers everywhere, the Sierra became a demonstration of the public understanding of science. (And, less positively, of Ford's misreading of the marketplace.) The science is straightforward: at speeds above a mere 60kp/h (37mph), aerodynamic drag absorbs more energy than rolling resistance. Drag is represented by CD, a calculation that gives an open parachute a CD of 1.35 (about as high as it gets) and a pure aerofoil section a CD of 0.05. An efficient saloon car aims at something in the region of 0.35. This was Ford's target with the radical Sierra, a mass market product designed to persuade the public of the status value of efficient penetration. Instead, the public read it differently and tabloids soon spoke derisively of a 'jelly mould'. The Sierra was designed by a team led by Uwe Bahnsen, reporting to Joe Oros in the United States, one of the many fathers claiming responsibility for the Mustang. Bahnsen bravely refused conventional market research. When the Sierra was tested (without identifying badges) in consumer clinics, a majority felt that it was more expensive than the $2,000 target price. But the research did not ask the same consumers if they would actually buy it. The Sierra enhanced Ford's reputation among sophisticates, but its cool commercial reception alarmed management and sent Ford back to a conservative design policy that lasted 20 years.

1982

Audi 100

The four rings of the Audi badge betray the company's origins in the incestuous Wagnerian complexities of German industry. Each ring represents an automobile pioneer: DKW, Wanderer, Horch and Audi itself, brought together under pressure from the banks in 1932 as 'Auto Union'. In 1958 it was bought by Mercedes-Benz, which in 1965 sold it on to Volkswagen. For a while, Audi survived as a subbrand of its Volkswagen master. Only slowly did it achieve an independent design integrity. As a result, Audi had an unhelpfully imprecise identity, a matter made worse because, as market research revealed, many consumers thought that the Latin name 'Audi' suggested the car was Belgian. It is good to be Belgian if you are a surrealist, a chocolate or a beer manufacturer, but if you make cars, it is better to be German. When Ferdinand Piëch, grandson of Dr Porsche, took control of the company, he determined to establish a new identity for Audi with a series of audacious 'technical events'. The 1982 Audi 100 was a

tipping point for Audi's credibility. Exploiting some creative cues established in experimental safety cars in the Seventies – the *Forschungsauto* — the Audi 100 appeared at the very moment when marketers had determined that explicit technology would give the product a USP, a Unique Selling Proposition. The 100 was superlatively made, sheer and streamlined, an enormous, but light and elegant, body covered advanced componentry. The windows carried pegs which ran in slides, providing nearly flush glazing. In addition, the 100, with its confidently sheer surfaces and overt functional intelligence, established an Audi design language that lasted a quarter of a century. Its drag coefficient was 0.30. To emphasize its essential German character, the advertising agency Bartle Bogle Hegarty wrote the ineffable Eighties copyline 'Vorsprung durch Technik' and gave Audi brand values whose appeal had a near-erotic intensity for the new money of the decade.

Renault Twingo

At Renault, Patrick Le Quément persuaded Raymond Levy that research showing that 25 per cent of respondents disliked the Twingo concept should be ignored. His argument was, 'The biggest risk is to take no risk.' In time, the Twingo changed the popular conception of the small car: it was, in a phallocentric world, gender-neutral and in its design Le Quément bravely played with the symbolism and palette of the toy box. The Twingo jumped the species barrier and became an enjoyable product, rather than a prosthetic sexual device.

'As designers, we are in a fight between sheer seduction and image building,' Le Quément explained. 'A design statement that brings immediate returns but does not build the brand is a mistake.' The Twingo was launched at the Paris Salon of 1992; simultaneously, Renault refreshed its corporate graphics. Instrumentation was minimal, clutter eschewed. Rear seats slid and the package was gasp-making: a foot shorter than the Clio, Twingo had more space than a Renault 25. It was commercially interesting, too: price was kept down (to 55,000FR) because the only option was colour. Here Le Quément was characteristically contrarian: at a time when white was overwhelmingly the most popular colour for French cars, Twingo was not available in it. Instead, the palette included swamp green, Latvian hooker purple, bubble-gum pink and parrot-dropping brown. Despite its celebrity, the Twingo was never taken up by youth: it was a strange example of radical design appealing to the middle-aged.

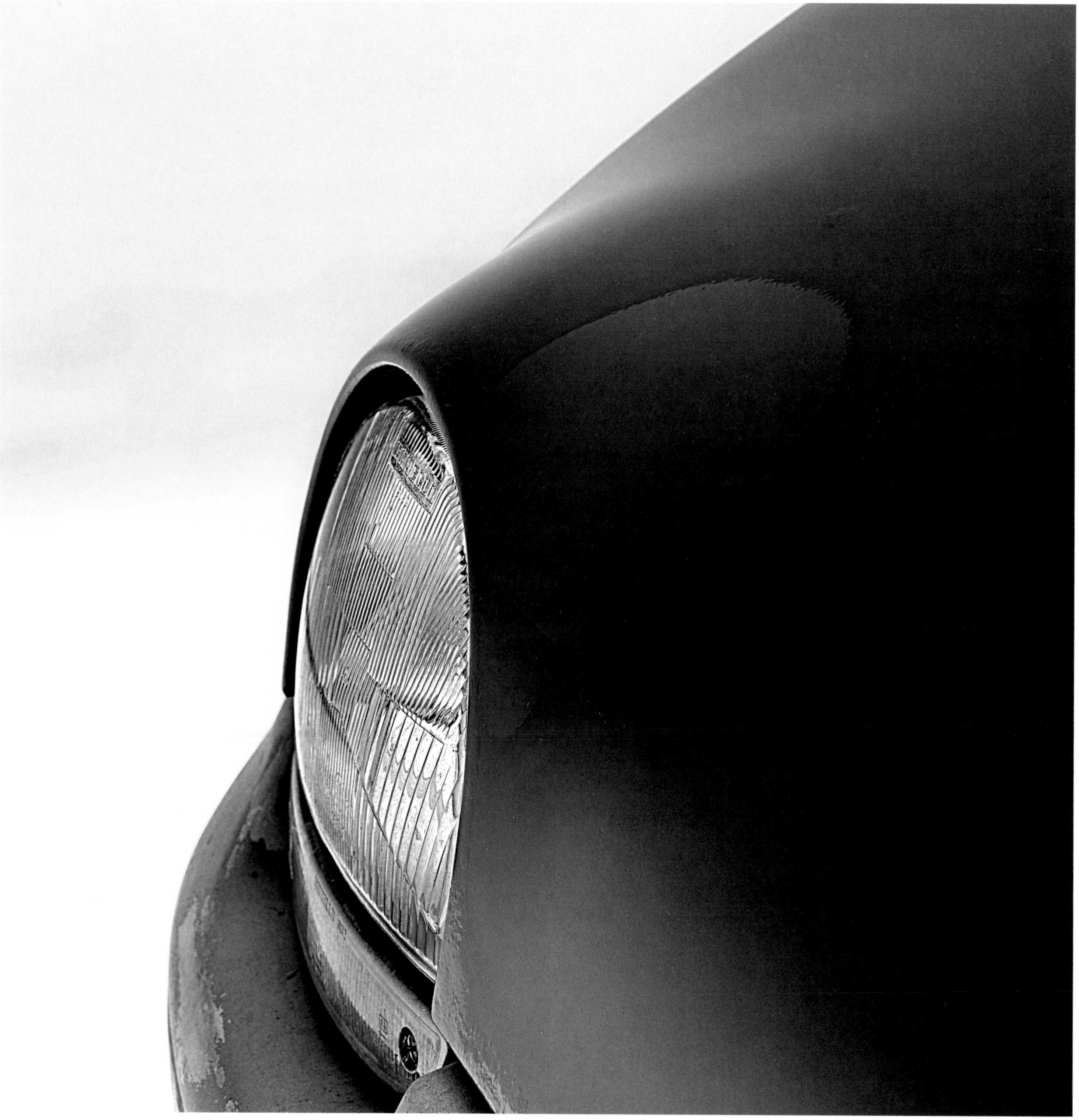

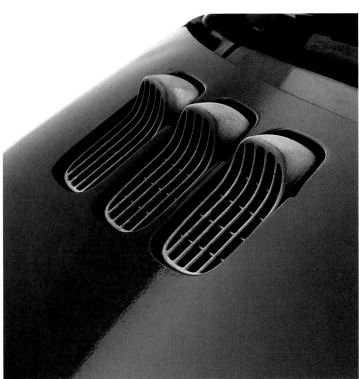

1998

smart

In 1994 Daimler-Benz and Swatch (in fact, Schweizerische Gesellschaft für Mikroelektronik und Uhrenindustrie), the novelty watch manufacturer, announced a joint venture to produce a Swatchmobile. Daimler-Benz's reputation had been made with peerless technology and benchmark quality; Swatch's by a radicalization of the stuffy Swiss watch industry and an offer to the consumer which included defiantly un-Swiss characteristics including, funk, sex, new materials and humour. This rich and bizarre concatenation of influences created the first car to establish a new format since Alec Issigonis' Mini of 1959. Early development was in California, under a team led by Gerhard Steinle. The Swatchmobile, now rebranded smart (the lowercase 's' is insisted on by the manufacturer's stylebook) rolled out on 2 October 1998. With an overall length of 2.5m (8ft), it was promoted not as a car but as a new urban transport system. It was sold through standalone smart centres. Early PR spoke of 'a new, modular, partner-based production process'. The architecture of smart was defined by an ultra-strong and visually emphatic steel frame with eco-friendly powder paint. Panels were made of recycled plastic, easily replaced. The potential for an amusing modularity existed, but was never fully exploited. The smart's packaging was extraordinary: a tiny three-cylinder engine mounted below floor level at the rear allowed accommodation for two passengers with similar space and amenity to a mid-sized saloon. Consumers were at first perturbed. And as early models had stability problems (caused by a very short wheelbase and a very high centre of gravity), these consumers became even more perturbed. But eventually the extraordinary convenience and charm of the car won sceptics over. Consumers enjoyed its strange mixture of eccentricity and very high levels of physical quality. Both practically and artistically, a new language was established. When a second-generation smart appeared in 2007, it was merely a development of the original. More a consumer product than an automobile, a smart is on exhibit in the design collection of New York's Museum of Modern Art.

Renault Avantime

Patrick Le Quément is bilingual, but he uses French to explain *'épanouissement de l'esthétique de la signature'*. The Avantime (a name which proved as elusive in pronunciation as in meaning) was shown as a concept at the Geneva Salon of 1999. Its purpose was to demonstrate, against the background of somewhat staid reality, Renault's culture of innovation. Its aim was no less than to redefine the architecture of the car for the new millennium. Proportions are curious: a single volume with thrusting snout at the front, a pert bottom at the rear. The rear window is vertical in side elevation but rounded in plan, helping to achieve a sense of dynamism, if not positive aesthetic unease. Large wheels gave the car an imposing stance, but it was the apertures that made the car remarkable. All the side glass retracted in this pillarless coupé with a full-length glass roof. Exceptionally large doors travelled on a twin-stage mechanism making access easy but minimizing the arc of travel. Inside, the furnishings were four imponderably large chairs, as if in an avant-garde Bentley. The Avantime went into production in 2001 but it was not, according to Le Quément, 'well born'. Problems in manufacturing a demanding specification led to delays and, in turn, these led to quality problems experienced by the few customers bold enough to bet on a concept. Despite, or perhaps because of, its outstandingly innovative character, the Avantime was a commercial failure: sorry evidence that it is not prudent to test Raymond Loewy's principle of MAYA ('most advanced yet acceptable'). While it remains one of the outstanding car designs of all time, the Avantime's tribulations forced Renault's management on to a course of conservatism.

2002

Nissan Cube

Shiro Nakamura, Nissan's Chief Designer, has said, 'It is our task to ask how to make the car more exciting, more expressive and more attractive.' So he designed a car apparently modelled on a paediatric psychologist's Froebel block. The overture to the Cube was the Chapeau concept of 1989 and the Chappo concept car, first seen at the Geneva Salon de l'Automobile in 2001. Nakamura cites a strong inspirational link to the formalism of traditional Japanese culture, but the Cube also draws on more recent and frequently eccentric Japanese design traditions. Nissan has a happy tradition of specializing in high-concept, low-volume genre cars with a retro-futuristic feel: the Be-1 of 1985, the S-Cargo of 1987 and the Figaro of 1989, all the products of a consultant 'conceptor', each one a shock to the system and an amusing affront to convention. The Cube is a confident development of these experiments. The Japanese have no very great tradition of sculpture in the round but excel at graphics. The Cube is thus like a diagram composed of straight lines and right angles, mediated by understated and disciplined curves. It is odd, uncompromising, innovative and exceptionally efficient in terms of space utilization. Publicity photographs showed Nakamura posing with Cube in the Omotesando district of Tokyo, the centre of the Japanese fashion industry, as if to emphasize that the Cube had more in common with fashion accessories or an iPod than with an automobile.

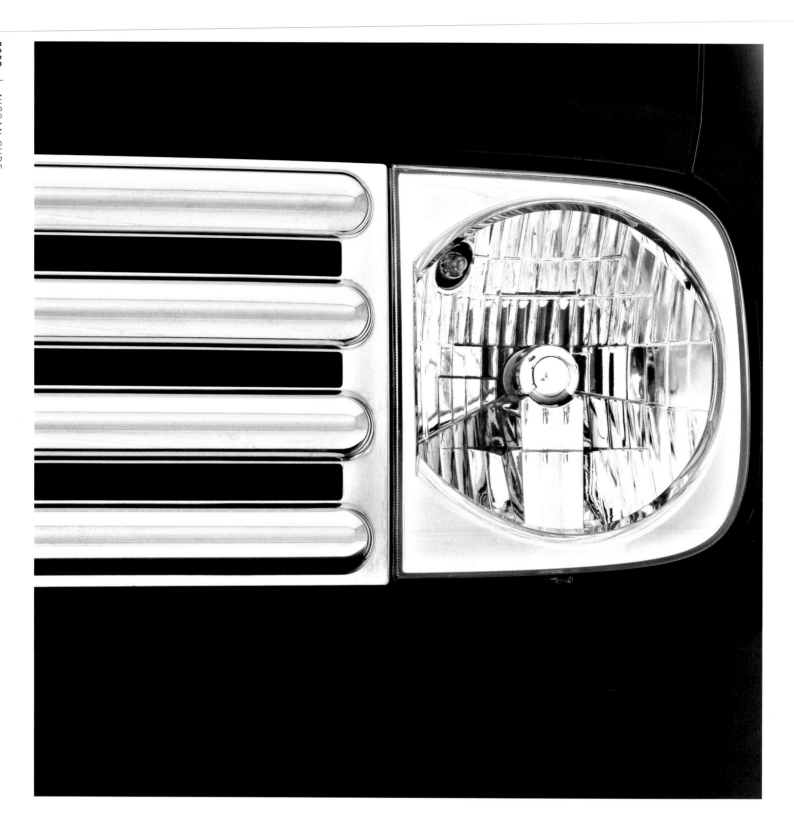

2003

BMW 5

BMW's traditional refusal of frivolous change cleverly demonstrated an essential belief in the rightness of its design whose language was established nearly 40 years ago by Paul Bracq. In this way, BMW told its customers they were doing the right thing: buying a BMW was more like joining an evangelical sect which worshipped handsome and understated design. In 2003 BMW decided on radical change. In the conservative world of car design, this was a disruption that may be compared to Picasso's creation of Cubism. The new design direction, originally described as 'flame surfacing', was controversial: in place of good proportions there is imbalance; thoughtful details have been replaced by baroque flourishes; a sense of rationality has been usurped by wilful expressiveness; calm sobriety has been blinded and deafened by a reckless taste for tactile instability and graphic fidgetiness. While this alienated many established customers, it was partly justified by changing demographics; Chinese and Indian markets are less tolerant of BMW's gentility. Chris Bangle says, 'It is the most avant-garde thing BMW has ever done. When that thing is in front of me, I just want to follow it.'

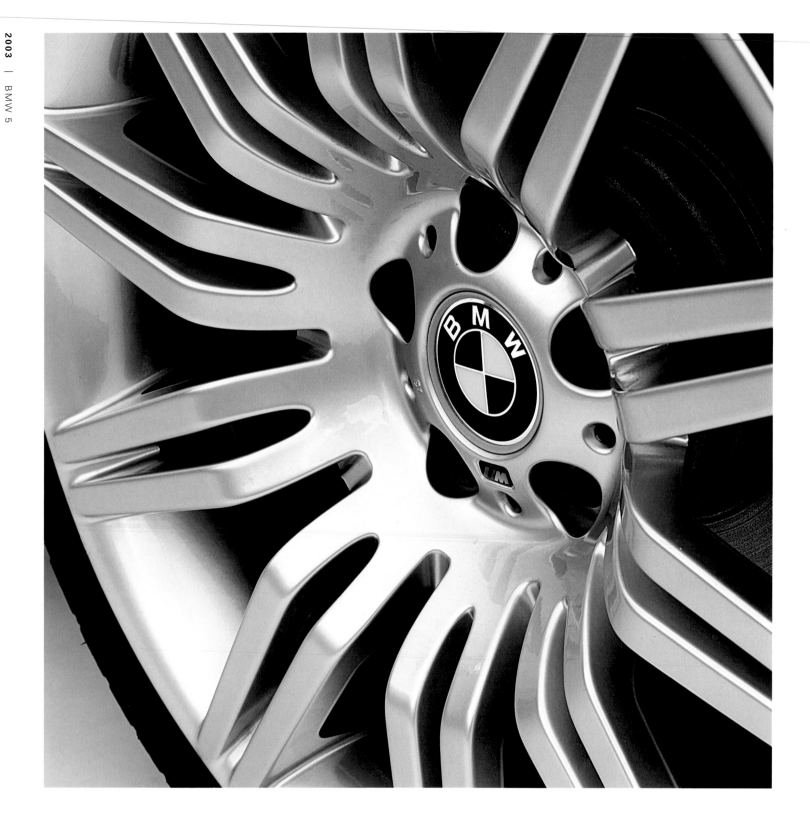

Were an Alien Visitor
To hover a few hundred yards above the planet
It could be forgiven for thinking
That cars were the dominant life-form,
And that human beings were a kind of ambulatory fuel cell,
Injected when the car wished to move off,
And ejected when they were spent.

Heathcote Williams, 1991.

Acknowledgements

PAGE 34–37

Ford Model T
Mike Vidler

PAGE 38–41

Citroën 11CV Traction Avant
John Gilroy White

PAGE 42–45

Lincoln Zephyr
Colin Sprong

PAGE 46–49

Chrysler Airflow
Brook Classic
www.brook-classics.co.uk

PAGE 50–53

BMW 328 Mille Miglia
BMW

PAGE 54–57

Jeep
Dallas Auto Parts
www.dallasautoparts.com

PAGE 58–61

Cisitalia
Abraham Kogan

PAGE 62–65

Cadillac '61
Kevin Nolan
k.pd@virgin.net

PAGE 66–69

Jaguar XK120
Classic Chrome Ltd
www.classic-chrome.co.uk

PAGE 70–73

Land Rover Series I
DK Engineering
www.dkeng.co.uk

PAGE 74–77

Porsche 356
Maxted Page
www.maxted-page.com

PAGE 78–81

Citroën 2CV
Jeff Colmer

PAGE 82–85

Volkswagen
John Maxwell

PAGE 86–89

Ford
Robert van Boesschoten

382 | ACKNOWLEDGEMENTS

PAGE 202–205

Cadillac Eldorado Biarritz
Mark & Pip Sumpter
www.paragon.gb.com

PAGE 206–209

Lincoln Continental
Ciaran Payne

PAGE 210–213

Jaguar E-Type
John Creed Miles

PAGE 214–217

BMW 1500
BMW

PAGE 218–221

NSU Prinz
Rob Talbot

PAGE 222–225

Alfa Romeo Giulia
Jeremy Brown

PAGE 226–229

Renault 4
Tim Jackson

PAGE 230–233

Lancia Flavia Zagato
Bill Amberg

PAGE 234–237

Ford Cortina
Brain Raymond

PAGE 238–241

Porsche 911
Maxted Page
www.maxted-page.com

PAGE 242–245

Buick Riviera
Classic Car Club
www.classiccarclub.co.uk

PAGE 246–249

Rover P6
Nick Dunning

PAGE 250–253

Mercedes-Benz SL
Classic Chrome Ltd
www.classic-chrome.co.uk

PAGE 254–257

Chevrolet Corvette
Pat Fitzgerald

PAGE 258–261

Panhard 24CT
Brian Oswald

PAGE 262–265

Ferrari 250GTO
Nick Mason

PAGE 266–269

Ford Mustang
Classic Car Club
www.classiccarclub.co.uk

PAGE 270–273

Pontiac GTO
Tim Arrowsmith

PAGE 274–277

Toyota 2000GT
Robert Close

PAGE 278–281

Oldsmobile Toronado
Spurr Cars
www.americancarsuk.com

PAGE 282–285

Toyota Corolla
Dave Dawson

PAGE 286–289

Volvo 144
Gillian Whitton

PAGE 290–293

Alfa Romeo Duetto Spider
Richard Rees

PAGE 294–297

NSU Ro80
Vincent Demarest

PAGE 298–301

Alfa Romeo Montreal
Rob Jones

PAGE 302–305

Ferrari Daytona
DK Engineering
www.dkeng.co.uk

PAGE 306–309

Jaguar XJ6
Paul Duce
www.classics-cabriolets.co.uk

PAGE 310–313

Citroën SM
Paul Duce
www.classics-cabriolets.co.uk

The publisher would like to thank the following contributors for their kind permission to reproduce the photographs in this book.

10 Fonds Doisneau/Collection Renault, France;13 above Fonds Doisneau/ Collection Renault, France;13 below 6487/Gamma/Camera Press London; 14 Sanford H.Roth/Seita Ohnishi/Rapho/ Camera Press London;15 Louis Faurer, Courtesy of Mark Faurer;16 left Rossi-Siochan/Gamma/Camera Press London; 16 right Zoltan Glass/NMeM/Science & Society Picture Library;17 left Michael Ormerod/Millennium Images;17 right Zoltan Glass/NMeM/Science & Society Picture Library;18 above ©2008 Digital Image, The Museum of Modern Art, New York/Scala, Florence;18 below Car Culture/Getty Images;21 Aerialarchives.com/ Alamy;22 Keystone-France/Camera Press London;23 Keystone-France/Camera Press London;24 Pininfarina;24 below Elliott Erwitt/Magnum Photos;26 left Car Culture/Getty Images;26 right Jacques Henri Lartigue ©Ministere de la Culture, France/AAJHL;27 left Pierre Belzeaux/ Rapho/Camera Press London;27 right Farrenkopf/BMW AG Konzernarchiv; 28 Three Lions/Getty Images;29 ©2008. Digital Image, The Museum of Modern Art, New York/Scala, Florence;31 ©Walker Evans Archive, The Metropolitan Museum of Art (1994.251.482 Auto Graveyard in Field, 1933, Film negative 2½ x 4¼ in.)

Every effort has been made to trace the copyright holders. We apologize in advance for any unintentional omissions and would be pleased to insert the appropriate acknowledgement in any subsequent publication.

The author would like to thank…

All books are collaborative exercises, this one more so than most. First I must thank Tom Wolfe whose *The Kandy-Kolored Tangerine-Flake Streamline Baby* I read on my knee beneath a desk in school forty years ago. The book, like Tom himself, still inspires me. Indeed, it inspired our title, as textual sleuths will have noted. Next, the editorial, production and picture research team at Conran Octopus. Lorraine Dickey, Sybella Marlow, Sian Parkhouse and Anne-Marie Hoines were always exceptionally supportive, charming and efficient, even when nagging. Extra special thanks, however, to Katherine Hockley who handled a very complicated production without complaint. At least, without complaint to me! Jonathan Christie's superb design has made *Cars* even better than I hoped it would be. But the very special character of this book is due to Tif Hunter. His photographs utterly transcend the limitations of a sometimes trashy medium: Tif's pictures alone make the case for cars as works of art. And all of them were made possible by an ingenious travelling studio of Tif's own invention. But had it not been for Tif's indefatigable agent and producer, Sue Allatt, we would have had nothing to photograph. With very unusual and cheerful persistence, Sue found cars in sheds, airport hangars and suburban garages. She patiently negotiated access with all the owners who were, of course, the most important collaborators of all.

The photographer would like to thank...

In my case the debt of inspiration comes from one of my long-time photographic heroes, Irving Penn. With his book *Worlds in a Small Room*, he shot people from far-flung places in situ using a tent with a plain background. The design and fabrication of my tent was brilliantly executed by Andy Knight and Pete Jenkins. It performed brilliantly and coped without a hitch despite all that the English weather threw at it. The erection of said tent, car cleaning and all the other photography-related duties were ably carried out by a team of assistants that included Jared Price, Dave Mitchell, Scott MacSween, Jasper Hunter, Emma Tunbridge, Enda Bowe, John Wilson, Liz McBurney, Tom East, Klaus Madengruber, Stuart Hendry, Fraser Lawson, Tom Andrew, Graham Wardale, Luke aan de Weil and Joe Giacomet. My agent, Sue Allatt deserves a medal for sourcing all the cars and I know she would like to thank Mike Hallowes of Ten Tenths for his invaluable knowledge and assistance. I'd also like to thank Jonathan Christie from Conran Octopus for asking me to be involved in this project in the first place. To see and touch such an array of beautiful cars and to meet their owners has been a pleasure and a privilege.

The publisher would like to thank...

Peter Jones (www.fiatpandaclub.co.uk), Billy Roe (www.northamericanmotorco.com), The boys at Classic Car Club (www.classiccarclub.co.uk), Andy Craig at *Classic American* magazine (www.classic-american.com), Savo at Clerkenwell Motors (www.clerkenwellmotors.co.uk), Ted Bemand, RM Auctions (www.rmauctions.com), Arthur & Elieen Melrose, The Historic VW Club, Gavin Ward at BMW, Audi UK, Volkswagen, Julian Balme, Robert Coucher at *Octane* magazine, Ricky James, Eddy Pearce, Foxy, South Western Vehicle Auctions, Pontiac Drivers Club, Yorkshire Motor Musum.